SOCIAL OPPRESSION

Recent Titles in
Contributions in Sociology

SOCIAL OPPRESSION

Adam Podgórecki

Contributions in Sociology,
Number 106
Marvin Wolfgang, *Series Adviser*

GREENWOOD PRESS
Westport, Connecticut • London

Library of Congress Cataloging-in-Publication Data

Podgórecki, Adam.
    Social oppression / Adam Podgórecki.
       p.   cm. — (Contributions in sociology, ISSN 0084–9278 ; no.
    106)
    Includes bibliographical references and index.
    ISBN 0–313–29024–5 (alk. paper)
    1. Oppression (Psychology) 2. Social psychology. 3. Law—
    Psychological aspects. 4. Sociological jurisprudence. I. Title.
    II. Series.
    HM271.P56   1993
    302—dc20   93–7712

British Library Cataloguing in Publication Data is available.

Library of Congress Catalog Card Number: 93–7712
ISBN: 0–313–29024–5
ISSN: 0084–9278

First published in 1993

Greenwood Press, 88 Post Road West, Westport, CT 06881
An imprint of Greenwood Publishing Group, Inc.

Printed in the United States of America

The paper used in this book complies with the
Permanent Paper Standard issued by the National
Information Standards Organization (Z39.48–1984).

10 9 8 7 6 5 4 3 2 1

Contents

Preface

The origin of this book is connected with my intellectual links with several "invisible colleges." I have been associated with the Research Committee of Sociology of Law of the International Sociological Association (ISA) as a cofounder, vice president, and board member since 1962. The main intellectual task of this committee has been to investigate how normative aspects of social reality are apprehended by people in various countries and cultures, as well as to inquire into complex interrelationships between law, in its various forms, and other aspects of social, political, and economic life. I have also been associated with the ISA Research Committee of Sociotechnics (as its founder, first president, and board member) since 1973. This committee has been striving to find out how social change is envisioned by various social actors, what strategies are used in practical efforts to bring about desired social transfigurations, and what can be learned from historical examples of "dark" social engineering. I have been involved as well in the work of the ISA Research Committee of Sociology of Deviance and Social Control since 1970. Finally, I have been a member of the Research Council of ISA since its inception in 1966. The task of this council has been to stimulate and coordinate undergoing investigations in the areas of interest of various research committees of the ISA. Discussions with colleagues from dif-

ferent countries, including Polish scholars and especially Professor An-
drzej Kojder and Professor Jerzy Kwaśniewski, helped me clarify several
notions that are analyzed in this book.

My own scholarly investigations as well as my intellectual connections
with the research groups just mentioned convinced me that the phenomenon of social oppression had been badly neglected by the social
sciences.

Many contacts and conversations with colleagues in the Department
of Sociology and Anthropology at Ottawa's Carleton University helped
to focus my interest; the fortunate idea of that department to press me
to give a course in criminology that concentrated on oppression provided
me with an opportunity to test my ideas in my lectures and seminar
discussions. Moreover, I profited greatly from the presence of Tadeusz
Grygier, Professor Emeritus of the University of Ottawa, a notable author
and authority on the subject of social oppression.

Finally, I would like to mention the fact that in my recent published
work on theory in the sociology of law, *A Sociological Theory of Law*, law
is analyzed as petrified oppression, thus providing an intellectual background to some of the themes developed in the present volume.

I also wish to express my deep thanks to Ms. Claire Gigantes for her
most imaginative and efficient editorial help, to Professor Jon Alexander
for his enlightened interventions, Mr. Robert Hay for his remarks, and
to Anne Kiefer, my editor from Greenwood for her helpful comments.

SOCIAL OPPRESSION

Introduction

You must understand, therefore, that there are two ways of fighting: by law and by force. The first way is natural to men, and the second to beasts.

(N. Machiavelli)

SOCIOLOGY'S WHITE SPOT

The phenomenon of oppression has been studied by various disciplines. The problem of individual oppression, for example, has been analyzed extensively in psychology and social psychology. Many studies have been devoted to the phenomenon of psychological and physiological stresses, and many inquiries have been made into economic exploitation or political tyranny. Generally speaking, under a regime of economic oppression, victims are subjected to extortion of goods, labor, or services; under a regime of political oppression, the oppressed are subjugated to the patterns of institutional hegemony and dominated by those who possess power. In the case of social oppression, targets are pressured to yield to norms imposed on them. Why, however, has there been a marked lack of systematic inquiry into the problem of man-made social oppression, and why is the study of social oppression so neglected?

This neglect is all the more remarkable given that, in the 1960s, sociology was vividly preoccupied with the *conflict perspective*, which strongly criticized all hidden assumptions based on the idea of general social consensus. Ironically, this perspective kept as its own hidden assumption nonscientific, political premises according to which, first, the working class was historically exploited, and still is, by various parasitic social classes, and, second, the working class would emerge victorious and liberate society (and, eventually, the whole of humankind) from exploitation and injustice.

Recent events in Eastern Europe furnish a convincing lesson that this perspective was as biased as those it criticized. Nonetheless, without being aware of it, the conflict perspective was correct in its understanding that various social entities (groups, classes, strata) have been oppressed through man-made measures. This poignant observation should have been regarded as an issue of central significance in sociological studies and considered independently of political or economic exploitation—but it was not.

The following study attempts to fill this gap in sociological inquiry. Historically speaking, although the phenomenon of oppression has been ubiquitous, an arbitrary decision has been made to limit the present analysis to its modern appearance only.

OPPRESSION

The type of oppression that is imposed by nature is well known. It consists of the pains of sickness, the weaknesses of old age, the various liabilities of the body (its limited capabilities, infirmities, or degenerations), and all such stress-causing factors. "Oppres'd with two weak evils, age and hunger" was Shakespeare's formulation of the more hostile effects of nature on humans (*As You Like It*, act 2, scene 7, line 132). Studies in the area of natural sciences successfully analyze the whole kaleidoscope of these effects. Similarly, the social sciences have developed a "sociology of disasters," which describes and analyzes behavior caused by natural factors.[1]

Man-made oppression, however, is of a different character. Whereas "natural" oppressions are overt and easily recognizable, man-made—or socially induced—oppression has, as a rule, to be unmasked, even though in social life, oppression, like power, is ubiquitous. Moreover, unlike naturally induced oppression, the concept of man-made oppression accepts as its basic assumption the concept of *free will*. The existential idea that an individual can be the "master of his fate," or even that he/she is "sentenced to freedom," radically alters the perception of human-made oppression from the traditional notion that the human condition is one of pain and the creation of pain.

The circumstances of war, which are richest in oppressive situations and experiences (although of a special character), can be used to illustrate the complicated accumulation of factors that usually accompany an oppression in which not only individuals but also the whole social group is involved. On March 16, 1968, the U.S. army's Charlie Battalion killed about four hundred villagers, mostly women and children, in My Lai, Vietnam. The individual soldiers acted on the basis of free will. Nonetheless, they accepted orders received from their superiors. Though some of the soldiers had strong moral objections to fulfilling this oppressive order, the soldiers themselves had been frustrated and oppressed by several factors: (1) they had been unable for a long time to find the enemy and were engaged as a result in a ghostlike war; (2) the battalion had suffered numerous casualties from sniper attacks and booby traps having no military gains; and (3) while there was every indication that they would meet powerful Vietnamese resistance in My Lai, no military force was found there. This accumulation of various, sharply conflicting oppressions clearly generated a man-made oppression of a special type; however, it was the crucial element of command that came from legitimized authorities that was decisive in pushing these agents of free will to execute this tragic massacre.

There exist various valuable accounts of oppressive actions carried out by ordinary Americans in Vietnam; for example, Glasser's *365 Days*; Halberstam's *Making of a Quagmire*; or Taylor's *Nuremberg and Vietnam*. There also exist shocking accounts of the attitudes of ordinary Americans who directly experienced these events. In this interview, by Mike Wallace of the CBS News, a participant discusses the events of the My Lai massacre:

Q: How many people did you round up?

A: Well, there was about forty, fifty people that we gathered in the center of the village. And we placed them in there, and it was like a little island, right there in the center of the village, I'd say. . . .

Q: What kind of people—men, women, children?

A: Men, women, children.

Q: Babies?

A: Babies. And we huddled them up. We made them squat down and Lieutenant Calley came over and said, "You know what to do with them, don't you?" And I said yes. So I took it for granted that he just wanted us to watch them. And he left, and came back about ten or fifteen minutes later and said, "How come you ain't killed them yet?" And I told him that I didn't think you wanted us to kill them, that you just wanted us to guard them. He said, "No. I want them dead." So—

Q: He told this to all of you, or to you particularly?

A: Well. I was facing him. But the other three, four guys heard it and so he stepped back about ten, fifteen feet, and he started shooting them. And he told me to start shooting. So, I started shooting, I poured about four clips into the group.

Q: You fired four clips from your . . .

A: M16.

Q: And that's about how many clips—I mean, how many—

A: I carried seventeen rounds to each clip.

Q: So you fired something like 67 shots?

A: Right.

Q: And you killed how many? At that time?

A: Well, I fired them automatic, so you can't—you just spray the area on them and so you can't know how many you killed 'cause they were going fast. So I might have killed ten or fifteen of them.

Q: Men, women, and children?

A: Men, women, and children.

Q: And babies?

A: And babies (Mike Wallace interview on CBS News, *New York Times*, Nov. 25, 1969).

This tragedy contributed to the development of American jurisprudence. Steiner, in his review on war crimes and command responsibility, writes:

> The report by General William R. Peers and his commission listed a number of officers, including two generals, who may have failed to perform their duty. But only two officers were actually tried before military courts, and only one, Lieutenant William Calley, was convicted. In the case of Lieutenant William Calley, questions of knowledge did not arise, since Calley was charged with ordering his men to kill civilians, and with having participated in these killings. But they were raised in the case of Captain Ernest Medina, Calley's immediate superior.

A new standard in evaluating the concept of command responsibility was established by the judge. According to that standard: "The commander must have known (e.g., because of physical presence at the scene, as was the case of Medina) or should have known what was not sufficient for a conviction, but that actual knowledge was required" (Steiner 1985: 298).

This book is concerned exclusively with man-made oppression, which is usually understood as the "unjust or cruel exercise of authority or power" according to *Webster's* 1980 edition. From a theoretical point of view, this definition has only one virtue—it is short. Otherwise, it has at least three basic weaknesses: (1) it includes unclarified value judgments ("unjust," "cruel"); (2) it refers mainly to a commonsense understanding of the concept and thus accepts as valid different meanings that appear in different social settings; and (3) it uses logical disjuncture twice, thus providing room for semantic confusion.

Some attempts to formulate a definition of oppression read like the outline of a novel:

> Oppression is, above everything else, a condition of being, a particular stance one is forced to assume with respect to oneself, the world, and the exigencies of change. It is a pattern of hopelessness and helplessness. People only become oppressed when they have been forced (either subtly or with obvious malice) to finally succumb to the insidious process that continually undermines hope and subverts the desire to "become." The process, which often is self-perpetuating and self-reinforcing, leaves in its wake the kinds of human beings who have learned to view themselves and their world as chronically, almost genetically, estranged. The end product is an individual who is, in fact, alienated, isolated, and insulated from the society of which he nominally remains a member. He and society are spatially joined but psychologically separate: they inhabit parallel but nonreciprocal worlds (Goldberg 1978: 2–3).

The recent work of Young is an interesting exception, for she uses the concept of oppression in a more elaborate and precise way, heavily influenced by a "soft" type of Marxism that is quite normative: "In its new usage, oppression designates the disadvantage and injustice some people suffer not because a tyrannical power coerces them, but because of the everyday practices of a well-intentioned liberal society" (Young 1990: 41). She suggests that there are five "faces" of oppression. The first, *exploitation*, is "a steady process of the transfer of the results of the labour of one social group to benefit another." For example, exploitation could be based on the oppression of women, or on manipulation of conditions related to race or menial labor. The second, *marginalization*, is "the most dangerous form of oppression." It has mainly a material form and is, according to Young, a situation in which "a whole category of people is expelled from useful participation in social life." The third, *powerlessness*, is described negatively; Young argues that "the powerless lack the authority, status, and the sense of self that professionals tend to have." The fourth, *cultural imperialism*, "involves the universalization of a dominant group's experience and culture, and its establishment as the norm." The fifth and final face of oppression is *systematic violence* (Young 1990: 48–65).

Young believes that these criteria are objective. Her approach is based on an understanding that the main duty of the social scientist is to articulate the actual meanings of the basic concepts of the current social movements; hence she is not especially worried by semantical errors like *idem per idem* (tautology—"the same by the same"), the lack of precise definitions, or the usage of value-loaded concepts. This approach assumes some type of critical metalanguage and is not especially troubled by empirical evidence.

In contrast, I suggest the following understanding of oppression: it is an external or internal man-made limitation of the available options of human behavior of an individual or a group (if individuals belonging to this group identify themselves with it). This definition stresses that oppression may come from outside or inside. Oppression not only affects cognitive options of available types of conduct (these limitations may be especially visible when in contrast to a "revolution of expectations") and not only widens the options of human behavior (since it deals with legal and illegal attachments) but also restricts, sometimes in a literal sense, physical possibilities of behavior. Oppression is understood here not so much as a clear denial of expected options (which generates relative deprivation), or as a burden that seems to be obnoxious when compared with the light hardships of others (noticed due to relationship with other reference groups), but as a constant, invisible, almost unconsciously binding restriction of existing possibilities. By this perception, oppression may be treated as natural, given, or unquestionable. Since it is not always easily visible, it may appear for the individual as a result of a time of reflection.

Oppression can assume many forms: legal, economic, political, ideological, cultural, or existential. Kafka described, in an obsessive way, the oppressive entanglements of all forms that can enmesh an average citizen in his/her everyday life. Cultural pressures inside the bourgeoisie, and especially the lower-middle bourgeoisie, can be devastating, as Balzac and others have convincingly shown. Violations of human rights, as recorded by Amnesty International, indicate how vivid the problem of political oppression remains. Marxist doctrine was so obsessed with the liberation of the economically disadvantaged that it began to oppress even more severely those whom it was supposed to defend; however, ideological oppression, understood as a monopoly of accepted beliefs and the practices connected with them, is the essence of all totalitarian regimes and it is also the most comprehensive type of oppression.

SOCIAL OPPRESSION

Oppression usually descends in the wake of social struggle. If the struggle takes the form of a legal battle, its results are quite easily recognizable since they are reified into formal frameworks. If it takes the shape of a duel of opposite social or physical forces, then its consequences are, as a rule, multivariate, obscure, and laden with unexpected consequences. But oppression always manifests ongoing conflict. It appears when there are at least two adversaries enforcing opposite interests. In such a situation, the given level of oppression shows how far the oppressor can push and how much the oppressed can endure, indicating the relative strength of the oppressor and oppressed. In extreme situations, those who are oppressed may, in fact, be stronger; being aware of their potential, they may purposely restrain themselves from attacking until such time as they can demolish their opponents. As a rule, however, those who are more powerful suppress those who are weaker to keep under control latent or dormant conflicts. Therefore, human rights as generally proclaimed are not derived from "natural" or "divine" sources, but they are engendered by the type of oppression that is targeted against those who had aspired to these rights.

In the history of humankind, individuals and small groups move from the first stage of natural, concrete, face-to-face types of oppression and enter into the subsequent stage of abstract pressures applied through formalized social structures. In this stage, traditional means of social control such as the family, tribe, and community governance change their targets radically. Also, instruments for control of institutions, organizations, and various formal structures based on rational patterns of behavior replace traditional measures of social control. These new, rational measures of social control sequentially overwhelm human beings in a new and unprecedented way. Additionally, huge social superstructures, or macroexperiments imposed by the modern totalitarian systems, provide collective human experience with new instruments that are more suitable to the constantly shifting meanings of the globalization process. In these even more rationalized settings, the law starts to play a decisive role in shaping the image and reality of the "new world" and "new civilization." Thus, law and its pathology appear as the main instrument of social oppression. I shall return to this central point shortly.

Vulnerability can be treated as a good indicator of oppression. As Stanko (1987: 131–32) puts it:

> If we read the use of precautionary strategies as one indication of universal vulnerability, most of the research indicates that women feel more universally vulnerable than men. While, on the whole, individuals who have experienced some form of victimization have a greater tendency to change their behaviour to avoid future victimization, many victimized men do not seem automatically to alter their behaviour to protect their *physical* safety. Preliminary evidence from this ongoing research indicates that men are more likely than women to take additional measures to protect their material possessions—their cars or their belongings—rather than their persons, even if they themselves had been physically threatened or assaulted.

And, Stanko adds, also in a case of sexual assault, physical assault, or sexual harassment, "women adopt precautionary strategies as a way of living in a male-dominated world" (Stanko 1987: 133).

Once oppression becomes a matter of formal, abstract, and rationalized means of exerting pressure, social control enters into the psyche of an individual with an impact much increased by the creative ballast of technical and organizational social constructions. Human beings are more or less forcibly socialized to treat and absorb new technical and organizational surroundings as a natural type of environment. The essential feature of this environment is a transformation from external control of a body and its social habitat (attitudes, roles, status, etc.) into a new, internal, unprecedented reality of control. This control (or its pathological equivalent, ubiquitous totalitarian control) is implanted directly into the psyche of the individual, since it is the individual who is treated as the target of modern civilization. This advanced type of control tends to include in its pool of available measures the individual "I's," the selves of each given human being. In other words, it tends to incorporate as its strategic control measures those categories of self that are treated as the most treasured elements of human life. Thus, in effect, the individual is controlled not only from outside but from the very center of his/her existence—from within. Social control seems to be reified; it takes on a life of its own. To elucidate these problems better a task was undertaken to split the self, as an atom had once been split.

Empirical evidence that has been systematically accumulated tends currently to reshape old notions of justice, goodness, and rightness. Until now, social control of the first order (primary social control, that exercised inside small groups) and also of the second order (that exercised by the formalized schemata of social control) have been exerted in accordance with the dominant modes of social judgement of those social circles that have had the power to establish the main ethical norms. Consequently, all possible evaluations of the effects of social control of any kind have been determined by these types of standards. According to the new patterns of this emerging paradigm, social behavior in the area of social control is scrutinized also by a cognitive, professional, or scientific approach. This is control of the third order, or tertiary control. In other words, it is scrutinized by the expertise of those who become familiar with the socially established techniques of interaction—usually, those who are employed in various branches of the administrative and justice systems. But these techniques can be easily usurped by those who have power at their disposal.

FALSE CONSCIOUSNESS

Man-made or social oppressions do not necessarily manifest themselves (or become unmasked) through extraordinary or spectacular events. They can operate in the same way as the weather or air, perpetuating themselves in a "natural" way; they just exist. They have been generated by social structures that are established and reified by history and by the long-lived sociopolitical domination that has been supported by the well-organized and consistent apparatus of social control and repression. Even more, these oppressions maintain their existence with the continuous support of well-elaborated illusions that have been spread around by the phenomenon of *false consciousness*. South African *apartheid* is a suggestive example of such an internalized *Weltanschauung* that was able, in the past, to transform itself into ubiquitous, unquestionable "obviousness." Only recently has apartheid become the target of vigorous attack by more ethically sensitive whites.

> What used to be called the black problem has now become the white problem. It is not easy to accept that even in relation to the demise of apartheid, whites and their anxieties dominate. Justice would require that the central issue be how to guarantee that the oppressed majority's rights are restored and the effects of centuries of colonial and racial domination removed. Negotiations should be exclusively about how to dismantle the structures of apartheid, establish democracy, and correct the injustices of the past. Yet what is being projected as a central issue is the constitutional future of whites (Sachs 1990: 149).

Racial domination points to a significant ingredient of oppression, the very phenomenon of false consciousness: the inadequate and biased perception of the existing situation by an individual or collectively by a social group. Sometimes this perception can run contrary to the "objective" interests of those who generated it. Recent events in Eastern Europe unmasked several suggestive examples. A worker in a socialist country who lives everyday with socialism as it is and not as it is supposed to be, and yet who votes for the "socialistic" government that claims to represent his/her interests; or a social scientist specializing in problems of social stratification who provides his/her expertise for such a government—each is displaying a striking degree of hypocrisy. There are many reasons for this hypocrisy. Factors like greed, the desire for career advancement, the search for monetary rewards; or intellectual retardation, aggravated personal insecurity, authoritarian types of personalities: these, alone or in part, may play a decisive role here.

Economic and male-oriented types of oppression present further examples of successfully inculcated false consciousness. Women not only face the stress of physiological oppressions. They are not only placed in a stressful, disadvantageous position vis-à-vis men in domestic, social, economic, and political life; they are also deeply conditioned by ideology to do everything possible to make themselves pleasant to men. This man-made captive *Weltanschauung*, this semi-ideological orientation can be even more oppressive than many types of accumulated, hard-natured physiological and economic disadvantages. The idea of being a man's "pet," implanted into the psyche of women by the long-standing processes of acculturation acquired in some socioreligious circles, is, in effect, almost a natural existential status. An inquiry into the interrelations of a pseudofamily composed of a pimp and the women who work for him linked the structure of economic and paternalistic dominance thus:

> A putative and potential refuge to women responding to a dearth of licit employment opportunities and the glitter and economic potential of the street, the pseudofamily actually emerges as a heteropatriarchal mechanism whose character, organization, and context serve to depress further, rather than enhance, the life chances of its female members. Once a woman is "turned out" by the "man" and listed in the pseudofamily, she is enmeshed in a tangled skein of conflicting emotions and motives; "wives-in-law" vie for the coveted position of "bottom woman" and for the attention and regard of their "man" and the "man" schemes (in concert with other "men") to maintain his/her dominance and, above all, the profitability of the union. As female hustlers age, and as their criminal records lengthen, they become marginal even to this world of last resort. Traded as chattel, often stripped entirely of property in the process of exchanging "men," and finally disowned when competition from other more naive, more attractive, and more obedient women becomes too strong, street women find themselves doubly jeopardized by capitalistic-patriarchal structures that are pervasive in "straight" society and profound upon the street (Romeneskó and Miller 1989: 1090).

Women are here the targets of a triple, mutually reinforcing oppression: economic, social (as executed by the family, a social body especially treasured by them), and male (perpetuated both by individual males and by males as a collective category). Women are not only financially exploited, physically used, suppressed by an official and intuitive law (as "wives-in-law"); they are also dominated by the ideology imposed on them.

While various types of oppression may reinforce each other, however, they may also contradict themselves. To take an example from South Africa, as one specialist explains:

> When certain males are extremely disadvantaged, it becomes more difficult for women to recognize their relative disadvantage *as women*. The fact that white women enjoy the privileges associated with being white in a white supremacist society, means that many are unlikely to feel more oppressed than black men. Similarly, due to the extreme deprivation suffered by black people under the system of apartheid, black women are not necessarily likely to feel more oppressed than black men (Hansson 1991: 4).

This view is not always so, however. One of the most intriguing controversies arising in the 1991 Senate confirmation hearings for Supreme Court nominee Judge Clarence Thomas was the question of why Anita Hill waited ten years to reveal her version of events. K. Morton in *Newsweek* (October 21, 1991) presents this explanation:

> There is more than personal catharsis at stake in owning up to this long-suppressed incident. I am writing this not only because the memory would not go. I am writing because Professor Hill's voice moved me to do so. I wanted to say to the Senate panel, "Look, I know why she stayed on with a man who insulted her. So many of us have been there, not liked ourselves for it, but we have stayed." And there is another impulse to my speaking out now. If men and women alike pronounce such degrading episodes unacceptable, perhaps our daughters might be spared similar choices in their professional lives. No one should have to purchase job security at so high a price.

THE LAW AS AN INSTRUMENT OF SOCIAL OPPRESSION

As noted earlier, once concrete types of oppression are replaced in human society by abstract pressures applied through formalized social structures, the law becomes central in shaping the new order. Inside structures that are built on the basis of face-to-face interpersonal relations, this is done through the intuitive law potential (compare, Podgórecki, 1991: 37–67); inside institutional and organizational social bodies, this is mainly done by the services of official law. On the macro-level, or the level that combines the impersonal relations and requirements of institutional and organizational frames, this is done through the use of professional and cognitive measures. But all norms utilized by impersonal officials or rituals and etiquette have their roots in oppression that is socially established; is usually invisible and taken for granted; is sometimes despised, but is treated as natural; and usually is treated as legitimized.

Oppression is an independent factor of social life. As such, it cannot be reduced to economic exploitation, sexual harassment, racism, political intolerance, legal persecution, or other well-elaborated concepts. It is a social pressure that functions as an additional component generated by various natural and man-made factors. The experience of Native women, which was incorporated into the report on federally sentenced women in Canada, may exemplify these man-made factors:

> Our understandings of law, of courts, of police, of the judicial system, and of prisoners are set by a lifetime's defined racism. Racism is not simply set by the overt experiences of racism, though most of us have known

this direct hatred, have been called "dirty Indians" in school, or in foster homes, or by police or guards, or have seen differences in the way we were treated and have known that this was no accident. Racism is much more extensive than this. Culturally, economically, and as People we have been oppressed and pushed aside by the Whites. We were sent to live on reserves that denied us a livelihood; controlled with rules that we did not set and that made us dependent on services we could not provide ourselves (*Creating Choices* 1990: 19).

APPROACH AND OVERVIEW

The normative content of the law and oppression makes it imperative to find a special method of inquiry that combines an evaluative perspective with the requirements of the empirical approach. In this study, I have used what may be called a multidimensional approach to the problem of social oppression. Such an approach develops a complex methodological and conceptual framework that permits analysis of social issues from different perspectives, so that the various faces of social reality can be grasped more comprehensively. The essence of this idea was presented in the book *Multidimensional Sociology* (Podgórecki and Łoś 1979):

> It is not possible to see in the darkness a complicated structure unless it is illuminated from different angles at the same time. But when the light comes from one angle only, then the emerging vision would lack entirely the intriguing complexity of the whole. As a result this vision impoverishes the picture of the reality.

One of the central tools of the multidimensional approach is *social empathy*, a learned understanding of other human beings surrounded by the social world, an understanding of what belongs to the social world that is alien to a given individual. In other words, social empathy is an entrance into a world of social existence other than one's own; this entrance is accomplished by experiencing, whether directly or indirectly, other people's existential specificity. By this means, one can absorb different types of sociopersonal experiences that are different from one's own internal world.

Bergsonian intuition, Diltheyan procedure that furnishes the thinker with data pertaining to the external reality; Znaniecki's "humanistic coefficient," which supposedly allows one to grasp the specificity of others' comprehension of the world existing outside; Petrażycki's enlarged comprehension of introspection; and even Giddens's "double hermeneutics" (lay actors' meanings of social life and the reconstruction of frames of these meanings) should be treated as gradual approximations of the notion of social empathy.

If they are to be used in social practice, data obtained by the exercise of social empathy must, as a rule, be transformed into dependent or independent variables. To do this, they have to be husked from the mixture of existing matter and the flow of current events, and operationalized into constructs and notions suitable for empirical inquiry. Since in the process the data are deprived of their particular authenticity and uniqueness, it is advisable to flavor them with elements of everyday life, even anecdotes, to make their genuine character more visible.

STRUCTURE OF THE BOOK

A multidimensional approach is taken consciously here in an effort to counterbalance the strategy, currently so prevalent (especially among German and, to a lesser extent, British social scientists), of using almost exclusively abstract terms, putting them deftly, sometimes elegantly, into prearranged combinations, and supporting one empirically void statement with another void one as well. The multidimensional approach has its own shortcomings, however; it presents, for example, no new, shocking, unifying theory. Nevertheless, it discloses various often less well-known grimaces or poses of modern social reality. It also deals with the elusive phenomenon of human identification, which, recently blurred by the overwhelming proclivities toward omnipresent unification, has made a dramatic effort to reassert its singularity. Thus, social psychology undertook as its main task what was too multiplex for the discipline of psychology, and introduced a most adequate and comprehensive picture of individual self-vision. Positivism, with its inclination to testifiable and easily duplicated methods, had the job of squeezing out from its archives what could be said about social oppression in the form of proved generalizations.

The generalized and shocking experience of the twentieth century is put together in this volume not by normative-oriented condemnation, but by the rapidly growing discipline of the sociology of law. This critical study of law tries to find what is so efficient, diabolical, and commanding of obedience in the historically displayed totalitarian human ordeal. The study begins by examining those elements within human beings themselves that contribute to the efficacy of oppressive attempts at social control. The underlying contention of the whole of Chapter 2 is that the current understanding (independent of the postulates concerning relations between macro- and micro-) of the one-way influence of social institutions on individuals is inadequate: social systems are themselves influenced by the contents and structures of the various types of human "I's." It might even be said, metaphorically, that the pool of selves that exists in the given social system could be perceived as the superstructure. Moreover, the different types of selves are shaped by social systems in a circular way. To the extent that the selves are, indirectly, designed by the major forces of social systems, they also serve as *sui generis* puppets hidden behind these forces.

After presenting this self-oriented point of view in a subjectivist way, shorn of objective substance, it might be useful to confront the initial phenomenological perspective with positivist findings. Thus, Chapter 3 outlines various inquiries of particular relevance to the area of social oppression, which are supported by my own scholarly work on deviance as a professor of sociology on various continents (Asia, Australia, Europe, and North America). Additionally, I shall investigate whether the middle-range theory that is currently in use is appropriate for explaining generalizations of oppressed human behavior, or whether this theory needs some modification.

Chapters 4 and 5, dealing with totalitarian law, are the result of my direct involvement in professional work as a legal counsellor in postwar Poland, as well as my earlier underground fighting with German occupants and with the Polish government (see Podgórecki 1986). But totalitarianism has died and post-totalitarianism has been born. Hence, the perspectives of the political sciences, with their possible sensitivity to vivisection *in statu nascendi*, are used to elucidate those transformations of a specific post-totalitarian society—Poland, which through its heroic "Solidarity" movement,[2] set in motion the landslide of unexpected political changes in Eastern Europe and, subsequently, in the world. Chapter 6, in which a theory of the empirically oriented sociology of law is developed, capitalizes on the meteoric development of this new branch of the social sciences, of which I am a cofounder (Research Committee on Sociology of Law, 30 Years for the Sociology of Law 1991: 7).

Finally, it should be noted at the outset that totalitarianism is comprehended here as it is defined by Friedrich and Brzeziński: "The 'syndrome,' or pattern of interrelated traits, of the totalitarian dictatorship consists of an ideology, a single party typically led by one man, a terroristic police, a communications monopoly, a weapons monopoly, and a centrally directed economy" (Friedrich and Brzeziński 1965: 9).

In his foreword to Goldfarb's *Beyond Glasnost*, J. J. Szczepański notes that

two distinctive features of totalitarian ideology (whether it is of the leftist or rightist orientation) are the aspirations to create a "new man," and the quest for legitimization in the supposed will of the "masses." Here the cherished logical principle of the intellectual works according to its own (natural) rules. The concept of the "new man" inevitably adopts the shape of a docile subject of the regime, and the will of the "masses" is formulated by the ruling elite according to its political and class interests (Goldfarb 1989: x).

In this book, the *totalitarian system* is understood as a social system dominated by a homogeneous ideology imposed on society by a mono-party (one-party) and its oppressive apparatus. A *post-totalitarian system* emerges when the dominance of a monoparty has formally ceased, but while its deeply entrenched bureaucratic structure remains in place and the values, mores, and basic mechanisms generated under the totalitarian system still predominate.

NOTES

1. The synthetic summary of findings in this area stresses the following:

(1) Mass panic is a phenomenon that occurs rarely and only under certain circumstances; (2) few actual cases of looting can be discovered; (3) stricken populations are not a "dazed, helpless mass," but help themselves and perform rescue and welfare tasks; (4) the social group organization does not break down but is strengthened; (5) there are only isolated examples of breakdown of moral codes; (6) there is no significant increase in psychoses and psychoneuroses; (7) emotional aftereffects are widespread but relatively mild and transitory; (8) morale and optimism soon rebound and are abnormally high and transitory; (9) the big problem of crowd control is not flight of the victims from the disaster area, but a convergence of people to the disaster area from the outside (Berelson and Steiner 1964: 625).

2. Solidarity had five basic features: (1) trade union allegiance; (2) camouflaged ideology; (3) opposition to "official," cultural, based mainly on the Christian ancestry and human rights, ideology; (4) rejection of the Marxist concept of "class conflict" and acceptance of the idea of social unity; and (5) the idea of revolution without violence.

2

Oppression from Within

The self has returned! After almost seven decades, there has been
a resurgence of interest in the concept of self. At the turn of the
century, the self was a major tenet in many theories of human behaviour. William James, George Herbert Mead, Carl Jung, and a
score of other notable figures had elevated the self to a position of
primacy in their theories. But, by the 1920s, the influence of logical
positivism and other reductionistic movements had significantly reduced the impact of the self on social science theory, and the self
had disappeared as a fundamental concept among all but a few
psychoanalytic and phenomenological theories.

(Marsella, De Vos, and Hsu, 1985)

When discussing the problem of social control and oppression, one
thinks, as a rule, about such supervisory agencies as the police (including
secret police), courts, the bureaucratic apparatus, and power elites, as
well as about education, religion, and political ideology. Institutions of
this sort play various and important roles in performing supervisory
tasks and are, as a whole, complementary in their concerted effort to
bring people's activities up to the expected standards. Some of these
agencies use techniques that are quite visible and obviously repulsive,

whereas others use techniques that are subtle, attractive, and unobtrusive. Tortures and governmental promotions, the psychological poisons of vicious gossip and intrigue, flatteries and compliments: all belong to this kaleidoscope of strategies. Due to their visibility, pressures of this kind have been described in more or less detail by specialists analyzing the interrelations of humans in different social settings.

It is easy, however, to overlook the particular type of control that lies, hidden and unseen, deep within the human psyche. This kind of control relies on devices that are inculcated upon the human soul and that operate automatically within it; they can be more powerful than all the spectacularly oppressive or covert and seductive institutions that constantly impose social conformity.

It was Marx who highlighted the possibility of transforming oppression into self-oppression.

> It is necessary to make the actual pressure even more pressing by adding to it the consciousness of pressure; the shame even more shameful by making it public. . . . We have to make the ossified conditions dance by singing them their own melody! We have to cause the people to be *frightened* by their own image, in order to give them *courage* (quoted in Meyer 1957: 19).

What, then, are these inherent, hidden, invisible, unspecified, yet crucial forces of social control?

In order to identify these forces more clearly, one has to analyze the different types of techniques that ensure that social behavior conforms with the basic values of social order. One of the most important techniques of this kind consists of the implanting into the psyche of each member of society the appropriate type of social "I," or self.

An observation should be made at the outset about the basic concepts of self used in this chapter. In quest of an adequate classification of different types of socially relevant selves, I have developed my own, rather than trying to find and assess all possible antecedent understandings of the various types of "I." Thus, eight types of social selves are proposed here for consideration: the Instrumental, the Facade, the Looking-glass, the Principled, the Ideal, the Real, the Subsidiary, and the Private selves.

It is possible, however, to enumerate other kinds of social selves. Mead, for example, held that the self was divided into "I" and "me." The "me" was supposed to be that part of the personality of which the actor is aware, as it represented the internalization of generalized others. It was also supposed to represent the forces of conformity. The "I" was that part of the self of which the actor was unaware. He became aware of it after an action was completed: the "I" was the response of the individual to the organized attitude of the community as it appeared in his/her experience. Its response to that organized attitude in turn changes it (Mead 1934: 196). My own analysis suggests that the situation is more complex than Mead believed. What he attributed to "I" belongs to the Private "I," and what was, in his judgement, specific to "me" is characteristic of the Looking-glass "I." Of course, one may say that this amounts to a play of words. But the central issue is to find real senses that stick behind semantic definitions.

Elster (1985) proposes some additional notions such as "hierarchical self," "parallel selves," "split selves," and "infinitely fragmented selves." But these seem to be a multiplication of insufficiently operationalized concepts. Similarly, the concept of "existential self" proposed by Kotarba emerges as too abstract. He states, for example, that

> the following working definition of existential self is intended to display the relative fluidity of the modern self and to account for the internal as well as external manifestations of the process of making sense of one's being. The existential self refers to an individual's unique experience of being within the context of contemporary social conditions, an experience most notably marked by an incessant sense of becoming and an active participation in social change (Kotarba and Fontana 1984).

The classification proposed here is supported mainly by my own research data, which may be treated as a synthesis of research conducted through several years.

THE INSTRUMENTAL "I"

The classics of sociology display quite accurate intuitions regarding the Instrumental Self. According to Weber, one of the most important types of behavior is *Zweckrational*, or goal-oriented, behavior. Freund presents a succinct interpretation of Weber's understanding of this type of conduct:

> A statesman, for instance, will not decide to act unless his action is intended to open up new prospects and consequently has a meaning; accordingly, in so far as his conduct is rational, he weighs the foreseeable consequences and considers those circumstances over which he has no control and which might wreck his project, in short, he constructs an ideal type of his future conduct in the form of a plan (Freund 1972: 107).

According to Pareto (1983), the main characteristic of instrumental behavior is the ability of sentiments (attitudes) to design, to create combinations of various types of elementary behavior. The ability to set schemes, plans, programs, tricks and strategies is motivated, according to Pareto, by "sentiments of combinations": impulses to innovate, to be cunning or to be wily. Petrażycki (1985: 221) understood instrumental behavior as a teleological attitudinal tendency to achieve desired goals: "Intellectually-emotional motivation which includes images of the results of activities (active and passive) and emotions triggering the relevant behaviour we will call goal-oriented or teleological motivation."

Empirical research supports these intuitions. But to conduct empirical studies in this area, one must make several assumptions. I have elsewhere conceptualized the meta-attitude[1] of instrumentality as consisting of a synthesis of several elementary attitudes (Podgórecki 1978; Podgórecki and Łoś 1979: 70). These elementary attitudes include a disposition to suspend the spontaneous reaction to given social stimuli; an inclination to calculate possible losses and gains through the analysis of various possible behavioral strategies; a tendency to behave according to a subjective vision of individual interests; and a disposition to accommodate oneself to the existing state of affairs.

Instrumentality appears not always as a product of subjectively perceived reality. It may be, as well, a result of a series of complicated and sometimes painful interactions of many "objective" processes. A conference on slavery held in Oxford in 1985 came to the following conclusion:

> To summarise, the slave status and condition has been purely social condition—that of a social isolate, an outsider, a person without kin, a person subject to the complete and arbitrary authority of the master, a person who could be whipped or tortured or sexually abused, a piece of property, and, by virtue of the foregoing, an instrument (Blackburn 1988: 276).

It would be a mistake to think that the instrumental attitude is, as a rule, destructive or entirely individualistic. It may be constructive, as in the case of the politician who takes into consideration the well-being of a larger social body (which he may identify with, or treat as his/her "lobby"). It may be collectivistic, as in the case of a politician who chooses to sacrifice his/her particular interests in order to achieve some community-oriented, nonindividualistic goal. Nonetheless, empirical data show that the instrumental attitude is predominantly oriented toward privately perceived aims (Podgórecki and Kojder 1972). One may discern instrumental attitudes in various spheres, such as in financial activities, sex life, personal relationships among friends, organizational and institutional arrangements, or even dealings with one's own personal feelings. Instrumental personalities usually confine their manipulativeness to certain restricted areas of the psyche.[2] Sociological research shows that instrumental attitudes strongly correlate with being young, insecure, and maladjusted (Podgórecki and Kojder 1972). Indeed, youth is linked with a larger pool of accessible options (or options that are subjectively treated as accessible); the greater the insecurity or maladjustment, the more urgent the need to find suitable and reliable "arrangements for arrangements."

In times of accelerated social change and instability, the Instrumental self plays a leading role in guiding an individual through various obstacles and dangers created by modern conditions of social life. In these situations, an individual may be influenced by a "fiddling" attitude to survival, an approach that uses all possible ways to survive, including illegal ones. The individual may then be pushed into the more extreme state of "dirty togetherness," a new concept meaning that one may so habitually yield to the various corrosive influences of traditional social control, and so separate them from one's own ethical emotions, that they become transformed into new personal traits involving specific, perverse forms of loyalty. Such loyalty is additionally cemented by family ties, mutual fiddling services, and private transactions of a reciprocal nature. These transactions raise the possibility of mutual blackmail should the code of collaboration be violated by either of the hitherto trustworthy partners.

All such manipulative and instrumental ties tend to lead people to establish stronger forms of solidarity than do impersonal, rational relationships. Such solidarity in turn creates its own superstructure, which dominates the social system in which it prospers (Podgórecki and Łoś 1979: 202–3); Podgórecki 1987: 67). In the framework of "dirty togetherness," each institution, factory and organization serves, apart from its own production tasks, as a formal or semiformal network that provides a stable frame of reference for an enormous number of mutual, semiprivate services and reciprocal arrangements. This network, irrespective of its questionable productive efficiency, becomes a very precious cover scheme. It is clear that individuals who operate inside this system, legal or semilegal, will, after a while, start to support it, not so much because they accept it (because of its normative validity or its assumed inherent virtues) but rather because they have become familiar with it, with the rules of the game, with its who's who background and the conditions of efficiency it provides. Under the pressure of instrumentality, traditional attitudes may change their once-established meanings. For example, envy may become envy for its own sake, treated as a goal in itself. Envy may thus lose its original function as a negative regulator generated by the attitude of survival, which, in an anticipatory way, peeps into and undermines the skills and strategies of others, in order to prevent them from threatening one's own options (Podgórecki 1978: 162; Podgórecki and Łoś 1979: 240).[3] This concept also figures in the work of Marody, who says, "Envious egalitarianism . . . seems to govern attitudes toward people [in Poland]. This attitude is buttressed by the principle of social equality seen as the end rather than the starting point for the individual career" (Marody 1988: 102).

Different types of instrumental attitudes, like "dirty togetherness," the fiddling survival strategy, or the pathology of envy, provide various examples of the use or misuse of different kinds of social control. These examples show that individuals may be pressured into behaving in ways that conflict with their own values; behaving for their own benefit in a direction contrary to that which is indicated by the basic (primary and secondary) systems of social control. This is because a stronger system of tertiary social control enters into the picture with overwhelming force. Where primary social control uses the internal pressures of informal groups, and secondary as well as tertiary control uses the apparatus of the formal legal system, the fourth type of control takes advantage of the superstructure of the dirty togetherness network.

Berelson and Steiner's neglected synthesis of empirical studies on behavior shows how instrumental behavior tends to prevail in human activity:

> He is extremely good in adaptive behavior—at doing or learning to do things that increase his chances for survival or for satisfaction. . . . He adjusts his social perception to fit not only the objective reality but also what suits his wishes and his needs. . . . He avoids the conflicts of issues and ideas whenever he can by changing the people around him rather than his mind (Berelson and Steiner 1964: 663–65).

THE FACADE "I"

The Facade "I" is not well recognized in the social sciences, despite the fact that it operates constantly in everyday behavior. The Facade self should be regarded as an aspect of self that is designed to convey to others an intended impression.[4] If a mediocre scholar drops names or presents as his/her own ideas that belong to a person who is out of the country; if an insignificant member of a bureaucratic establishment walks ceremoniously and dresses ostentatiously; if a young man parades before a naive girl his seemingly unlimited range of possibilities; if a writer complains that his/her best manuscript was lost in a travel accident; if a "globetrotter" describes life in countries which he/she, in fact, knows exclusively from the atlas: in all these cases, the message one is faced with claims the existence of some fictitious features.

In social reality, people may use the Facade self as a device for communicating to others that their qualifications and connections provide them with unusual possibilities. If there did not exist individuals who seriously believe that they would have been able to achieve greatly, had unfavorable circumstances not intervened, and individuals who seriously believe that the facade that they present actually belongs to them, the Facade self would be regarded merely as a specific subcategory of the Instrumental self.

In certain instances, however, Facade selves appear in virtually pure form. In these cases, facade personalities will develop such strategies as keeping various reference groups apart. For example, they may avoid inviting their "brainwashed" friends into their family circles, where the friends might acquire, from those who know them better, a more realistic, and therefore lower, opinion of their talents and potential. Con artists use the Facade self in a masterly and manipulative way to deceive and to gain, whereas snobs exploit facade both to convince others of their assumed qualifications and also to reinforce their own shaky belief that these qualifications are genuine.

Facades may be designed both individually and collectively. A person may hint that his/her family has a royal background. A vicious totalitarian institution may also invent legends, pretenses, and myths suggesting that its representatives are not only legitimate heralds of the institution's ideology but that they possess, as well, various precious features that are necessary to the institution's membership (e.g., collective wisdom).

Facade is not only used with various degrees of conviction to pretend something or to claim something; it may also become a trap, a knight's armor imposing its rigid limits on those imprisoned in it. In this sense, a facade may create an oppressive, dogmatic straitjacket in which behavior is determined by the ideology hidden behind the manifest appearance. Of course, behavior may be inspired and regulated both from within and from without. Thus, the facade may be regarded as one of the most devious devices for keeping under strict control those who might try to escape from it. A facade that has not been internalized compels its bearer (due to the attractiveness of presenting it to others) to socialize himself/herself to its image, whereas the already internalized facade exercises its power automatically.

A social system that is able to use the facade device as a tool for keeping its members within the bounds of its regime is highly economical: it needs fewer external punishments, since to lose a Facade self is a painful penalty. To build and maintain a decorative facade for an obedient servant is a cheap endeavor for the experienced machinery of the state's enterprise: if a state's bureaucratic edifice excels at anything, it is the maintenance of its decorative facilities. The invisible, intrinsic genius of these systems that base their power on the development of facades as effective manipulative devices is effective indeed: snobbery is unusually cheap—its production might be multiplied practically without any costs, when the fear of losing face is painfully oppressive.

Totalitarian social systems and their legal systems use the Facade self to perfection. In these systems, facade personalities enjoy the performance of spurious activities that consist almost exclusively of representation, controlling, giving advice, and participating in actions that are, as a rule, nonproductive. Being nonproductive, they are not linked to any responsibility. Being free of responsibility, they are primarily devoted to leisure. Being leisure-oriented, they receive and give constant rewards. Being continuously rewarding, they are highly attractive. Since they are so attractive, much is expected and demanded of those chosen to perform them. To fulfill these demands, they have to conform. The burden of this conformity can be formidable.

The Facade "I" exists in all social systems, in all stages of historical development. Although the phenomenon appears in the most striking way in totalitarian systems, in which all types of spurious activities blossom, the most telling example of the Facade self comes from anthropological studies. The social institution of the *potlatch*, most widely practiced among certain North American Indian tribes on the West Coast, consists of a large and public distribution of one's property, which is done on the basis of anticipated reciprocity. There can be many reasons for this distribution. It can be connected with trivial events, such as the first time a baby's hair is singed, or with more important ones, such as marriage festivities. Nevertheless, the main purpose of the potlatch is the validation of any or all claims to social rank, done in such a way that the recipient of gifts has to return greater value when it comes to his turn (Barnett 1938; Codere 1950).

Of course, this institution could have an important production-stimuli value: one has to work very hard to put on a better material performance than one's predecessor. Still the element of compulsive theatrical show dominates the activities of the Facade personality. Potlatch could be regarded as an expression of the Facade self, and the interpretation of this impressive custom should not be influenced by its misinterpretation and sometimes oppressive treatment through the law and the police. As York observes:

> Many traditional Indian dances and ceremonies—recognized as a vital element in the native cultural and spiritual identity—were outlawed as a result of amendments to the Indian Act in 1884 and 1895. Sun dances, thirst dances, potlatches, and other native ceremonies were raided and shut down by vigilant police officers (York 1990: 264).

In summary, there exist three kinds of Facade "I": (1) the Facade that does not have any support in reality, as its bearer is fully aware; (2) the Facade that is partially fictitious and partially real; and (3) the Facade "I" that, although fictitious, is totally supported by the subjective conviction that it is real.

LOOKING-GLASS "I"

The Looking-glass self is directly connected with the Facade self. If a person behaves in a pretentious way, he or she is usually doing so in order to impress others. In this case, a person should have an adequate view of the way he or she is perceived by others in order to behave effectively. He/she requires a picture that encompasses all negative and positive by-products of his/her activities. If this picture is correct, he/she is able to assess the total impact of his/her personality on others. If a person is unable to assess this impact, then he or she may occasionally face serious difficulties. In short, the Looking-glass self provides a person with feedback regarding his/her ego-perception and the activities of this ego and allows him or her to determine whether the image of his/her personality matches its prearranged design. The Looking-glass self serves as a psychological mirror.

As expressed by Simone de Beauvoir in her splendid prose, "When I am with Morice I cannot prevent myself from feeling I am in front of a judge. He thinks things about me that he does not tell me: it makes my head swim. I used to see myself so clearly through his eyes. Indeed I saw myself only through his eyes . . . " (de Beauvoir 1988: 157). If a person is fully facade-oriented, then the Looking-glass "I" serves him or her as an indispensable means of assessing the effectiveness of his/her endeavors. If a person is only partly Facade-oriented, then the Looking-glass perspective supplies his/her personality with "eyes" that closely observe how he/she is moving in the labyrinth of the social world.

The Looking-glass self does not only play the cognitive role of informing an individual about the image that he or she is creating and disseminating. The information itself may be analyzed but may, as well, trigger certain practical effects. For example, intensive and persistent labelling coming from outside tends to change a person's perception of himself/herself. If the content of this intensive labelling is internalized (and subsequently absorbed as one's own) then the phenomenon of secondary labelling appears: a person starts to judge everything through the alien eyes that have been imposed on him. He/she starts to look at himself/herself in a way that was conceived by the label designers. If they wish to change someone, injecting into his/her personality points of view that are alien to him/her, this approach can be quite successful. Labelling theory, and especially secondary labelling theory as developed by Lemert (1951) gives many examples of this phenomenon.

Personality changes of this type may open the door to many sociotechnical possibilities. The potential for influencing human beings has been well recognized by social manipulators, who have not hesitated to introduce them into social practice. In Poland in the 1960s, so-called workers' courts were established.[5] These courts dealt with petty crimes and breaches of labor discipline. They had no authority to apply sanctions provided by the criminal law. The "sentence" of the workers' court had a limited value; one always had the right to reject it or to appeal to the ordinary court. The main punishment used by workers' courts was the pressure of public opinion. All coworkers had the right to participate in the courts' proceedings and were encouraged to do so. In this way, the Looking-glass "I" emerged as a highly visible target of the criminal justice system.

What were the effects of criminal policy of this type? As far as workers' courts were concerned, the effects may be summarized in the following way: What a person believes others think of him (the Looking-glass self or the "reflected ego," as Znaniecki used to label it) is one of the most personal, intimate, and precious values cherished by anyone. If the opinion of a group is mobilized to demonstrate disapproval of a person who, until then, had believed that he was positively valued by others, the person censured can experience a real shock. It can be said that in self-evaluation, one relies more on others than on oneself. A prison term or a fine does not necessarily influence the image of the reflected ego, since these censures are impersonal; public condemnation can exert a much stronger impact (Podgórecki 1974: 149–57).

Sometimes progress in sociology is based on new names that a subsequent generation of sociologists gives to terms for which earlier experts had different tags. The concept of the Looking-glass self, for example, was introduced to the social sciences by Cooley (1902), who stated that the self is formulated through the imagined reactions and appraisals of others. This concept was later elaborated by Mead (1934), who maintained that the Looking-glass self is, in the case of a child, determined by his/her imitation of the reactions of significant others and by their relations to him/her. The concept of Looking-glass self indicates that, when surrounded by the watchful eyes of others, an individual may feel the surveillance he or she is under so acutely that he or she loses the ability to behave according to his/her own wishes and needs. His/her actions come to be guided exclusively by the judgements of others. Generally speaking, this imposed value-captivity may be more effective than the concrete walls of a jail. In the study of the influence of various ideologies, the phenomenon of iron-bound captivity in a prison built on dogmas could perhaps help to explain why some otherwise independent thinkers have been so effectively caught in the net of obviously criminal ideology.

THE PRINCIPLED "I"

In the modern social sciences, the first discussions of the Principled self were connected with Weber's notion of value-oriented behavior *wert-*

rational. According to this understanding, the agent of his/her own actions is exclusively guided by personal convictions. As noted earlier, Pareto suggested that there exist aggregates of sentiments; they express, in Powers's succinct formulation, "stubborn adherence to established ways and insistence on the preservation of tradition" (Powers 1987: 41). Earlier Petrażycki had understood principled attitudes as those subjective convictions that are closely correlated to the norms that prescribe them (Górecki 1974: 11). Sociological studies of the moral and legal attitudes of the Polish population have produced substantial evidence to support these intuitions. The attitude *fiat justicia, pereat mundus* (independently of what happens to the world, justice should prevail) is typical of the Principled "I." This type of self accepts a given norm, at the same time disregarding all possible and probable by-products of the actions undertaken. The Principled self is totally immersed in the binding aura of obligation. Nothing can eliminate the validity of a norm that is regarded as binding, except a norm of a higher order or an agreement between concerned parties. Knights, monks, missionaries, and scientists devoted to their tasks are examples of this kind of strict morality.

It is clear that, in general, well-established social structures generate these attitudes, which support the existing distribution of power and existing hierarchies of values. Thus, disseminating attitudes of this type is another "cheap" social strategy: the attitudes automatically strengthen the existing structures. If these attitudes are accepted, then extensive persuasive activities to socialize people are not needed. But again, remember that the Principled self exists and operates in all social systems. Its validity is not restricted to one particular socioeconomic type of society. Principled selves may also appear in periods of transition. For example, during times of revolution, when the existing system collapses and a different one emerges, a group of dedicated revolutionaries may surface. Although they are manipulative and fierce when fighting among themselves, they are strict, uncompromising, and firm in the area of their basic dogmas and respectful of the fundamental axes of their revolutionary ideology.

According to the findings of Polish sociological studies (and one should remember that Polish society in the 1960s went through substantial semirevolutionary changes), older people and those who were free of symptoms of insecurity and maladjustment expressed strong attitudes of a principled character (Podgórecki and Kojder 1972). Indeed, those who seemed to be secure and adjusted tended to accept the situation as it was; they had no need to change it. The large majority of them adhered to the silent norms of "civil society," and the minority accepted norms produced by the sociopolitical establishment. Additionally, those who were older were accustomed to their habits and ways and were not eager to change their behavior.

These data suggest a paradox of a different type. Those who should be regarded as free of physical and psychological chains are nonetheless oppressed by a rigid armor of norms and convictions; they are tightly bound by their own beliefs and norms. Freedom and oppression are closely interrelated here. As Merton says (1968: 384):

> What is generally known but only fitfully recognized: the individual's sense of being "at one with himself" is often only the result of being "at one" with the standards of a group in which he is affectively engaged. The sense of personal autonomy does not *necessarily* mean the rejection of normative constraints by all groups.

It is easy to see that the Principled self constitutes a basis for a legalistic way of thinking and the basis for formalistic behavior. It is, at the same time, the crucial ingredient of the bureaucratic habitat. All institutions and organizations that are built on the basis of legally conceived notions accept, as their cornerstone, an attitude of obedience toward the law. And this is exactly the cognitive basis of the Principled self. In the case of attitudes of this kind, it is not only the way of thinking that respects legal logic and takes into account the interrelated structure of legal norms of different hierarchies and orders that is significant. It is important, as well, to recognize the emotional impulsion that pushes human behavior in the direction prescribed by the normative guidance of the norm. The Principled self tends to be unconditional, categorical, and full of respect for the fundamental understanding of law as the law.

THE IDEAL "I"

Strangely enough, the Ideal self, which can help to preserve human freedom and liberty, can also, by the nature of its demands, constitute one of the strongest forms of oppression. The Ideal self is concerned with an individually perceived vision indicating how one should be, and not how one is. The Ideal self is built on the most cherished human dreams of the most sacred moral values. It offers a given individual a particular comparative reference personality (or set of values), which has to be regarded as the highest living aim.

For a scientist, the Ideal "I" paints a picture of a disciplined, inventive scholar, familiar with all achievements in his/her area and fully competent in the relevant methods and techniques: in short, a person who aims at the greatest cognitive discoveries. If a person is religious, then the Ideal self presents him or her with a model of a saint who disregards all worldly attractions and strives toward eternal values. The politician or social leader sees a picture of an altruistic activist who devotes all his/her capabilities, time, and resources, to the process of creating a better life for others. Because the process of creating a state of well-being for others is endless, so is the struggle to become a leader totally devoted to the goodness of humankind.

The nature of the Ideal "I" is such that it excludes the possibility of fulfilling itself. Thus, instead of being a source of delight in realizing the most precious human dreams, the Ideal self becomes, in fact, a tool of a torturing nature. The Ideal "I" constantly repeats, "You are still not good enough; not only do you have a long way to go but, as a matter of fact, you never will be able to reach the end." The Ideal self may demand the very lives of those who are dedicated to it. It may ask for suicide from its followers. The Koran says:

> Believers! Shall I point to you a profitable course that will save you from a woeful scourge? Have faith in Allah and His apostle and fight for his course with your wealth and your person. That would be best for you, if you but knew it. He will forgive you your sins and admit you to gardens watered by running streams; He will lodge you in pleasant mansions in the gardens of Eden. That is the supreme triumph. And He will bestow upon you other blessings you desire: help from Allah and a speedy victory. Proclaim the good things to the faithful (61: 10).

Loaded with ideological values, pressure from the Ideal "I" can sometimes function as the ultimate form of oppression.

THE REAL "I"

The Real "I" (or the Material "I") deals with all material and physiological determinants that influence the life of an individual. Some people are healthy and strong; some are fragile and weak. Some are very skillful with material and practical tasks; some are unable to perform even the simplest mechanical jobs (it was said that President Richard Nixon, who was the master of superpowers politics, apparently was unable to open a medicine bottle). Some people are able to accumulate others people's experience (firsthand or secondhand); some are unable to store even their own wisdom. Some possess wealth; others are possessed by it. The Real self could conceivably be shaped exclusively by external, material, or economic factors, but a sociological study[6] conducted in the 1960s among millionaires showed that among small circles of their friends (also millionaires), the amount of accumulated gold did not transform a particular individual into a sociometric "star." Popularity and high ratings went to those who were lively and entertaining. Bad health puts iron chains on one's aspirations.

The Real "I," despite the heavy emphasis that Marxists place on material factors (and which they so highly cherish in their private lives), is still a sociological enigma. Especially little is known about how the human body influences various types of socially constructed selves. For example, links between an authoritarian personality and health are not well elucidated. It should be expected, contrary to popular intuitions, that the authoritarian personality is not housed in a strong, healthy human body. It may be hypothesized that the closed, almost sealed structure of the authoritarian personality serves rather as a shell in which a person hides when necessary to survive the troublesome events of life. Probably the lack of reliable knowledge about the links between the human body and the Real self is responsible for the popularity of Freud's fairy-tale reasoning, which pretends to elucidate processes occurring inside the human psyche. The popularity of Freudian ideas should be attributed rather to the rapidly changing social mores concerning sexual life in wealthy bourgeois circles towards the end of the nineteenth and the beginning of the twentieth centuries. When a bourgeois entrepreneur, who was compelled to work by the Protestant ethic, realized that he had finally become secure enough to explore ways of using his/her wealth, sex appeared as a new and ideal area of exploration.

It should also be remembered that the Real self, being one of the white spots in the social sciences (areas not investigated for unclear reasons), is constantly used as an important factor in criminal sociotechnics (social engineering). For those who have power, human bodies are, or may be regarded as, targets of punishment. The death penalty, flogging, torture, starvation, even solitary confinement (which seems to target the human soul) are employed in order to keep people in line. A special retributive principle is in use here: a particular crime should be punished by a specified portion of pain. Currently this portion of pain is resultant from several essential factors. Ignatieff lists some of them, stating that

> the increasing pressure of numbers has acted to aggravate living conditions in often outmoded and decrepit institutions. Into overcrowded facilities have been cast a new generation of prisoners, more insistent on their rights than any in recent memory. In response to these pressures, reform-minded administrators come, arousing intense antagonism and overt opposition among guards. The combination of population pressure, public disillusionment, fumbling reform, prisoner militancy, and guard intransigence has broken the fragile order inside the prison (Ignatieff 1978: xi).

THE SUBSIDIARY "I"

It is necessary to mention an additional type of self, which might be called a Subsidiary "I." This type of self is much more widespread than it might be expected. If somebody does not have a self of his/her own, in the sense that he/she has been unable to generate his/her own life-perspective; if somebody feels that the lives of others are more exciting than his/her own life; if somebody identifies himself/herself with the tasks that have been prescribed for him/her by others; if somebody regards himself/herself as a *vessel* for an idea, doctrine, or ideology, then this individual may accept an alien self as his/her own. From this perspective, however, very few people have their own, authentic, genuine, self-developed selves.

Most individuals, according to this perspective, exist as implanted combinations of elements derived from outside. These clusters of more or less coordinated elements are kept together by one or several leading motives, which link together a dispersed variety of adopted features into an apparent synthesis. Boris Becker, the well-known tennis player, referring to his rapid success, expressed the idea of Subsidiary self relatively clearly:

> My luck was also my damned misfortune, because the life that overwhelmed me afterwards simply could not be handled by a 17-year-old alone. I was continuously forced to play a role I did not want to play. It was a substitute life which identified me completely with tennis and which turned me into a person I'm not. . . . And that has been so for five long years. I can never shake off this Becker, not even after the work is done. Round the clock I am this guy with the famous blue eyes, always and always this guy who is treated like the mascot by the people (Mike Wallace of CBS interview, in: *Times*, 23 June 1991).

The Subsidiary self probably appears in abundance among those who are strong believers in a particular world view doctrine. One might expect, though only empirical studies can prove, that a great majority of believing Marxists are people with considerably inflated selves. The same may be said, according to this conception, of faithful Muslims, dogmatic Catholics, opinionated Jews, aggressive Greens, and so on. It is clear that the Subsidiary self is especially prone to development by means of "dark" social engineering. But it is less obvious that this type of self could also acquire some sort of autotelic (valid for itself) "independence" and start to use its accumulated potential in a totally nihilistic way.

THE PRIVATE "I"

Of the various selves, the Private "I" is, without any doubt, the most effective as an identifying symbol. And it is, at the same time, the most difficult to identify. The more this particular self is developed, the more its bearer should be regarded as a full human being. The weaker the Private self, the greater the extent to which the individual consists of acquired slogans, clichés, and stereotypes. The modern world is full of paradoxes. It is possible for a given society to be very highly developed from the point of view of civilizational standards, while at the same time being composed of one-dimensional individuals entirely deprived of the riches of the Private "I."

In connection with the content of the private selves, one may notice that men are materially rich but women are richer still. Although feminist theory, currently so fashionable, is strong in issuing critical statements and is heavy in rightful, postulative demands, it makes few substantive statements about the nature of human reality of its own. One especially pertinent statement that it does make concerns the role of empathy in women's and men's lives. According to this view, women have a more strongly developed intuitive-cognitive ability to empathize:

> Empathy is built into their primary definition of self, and they have a variety of capabilities for experiencing another's needs or feelings as their own. Put another way, girls, because of female parenting, are less differentiated from others than boys, more continuous with and related to the external object world. They are differently oriented to their inner object world as well (Hartsock, summarizing ideas of Chodorow 1987: 167–68).

Feminist studies and some antifeminist ones have brought out many examples that may fortify this point. But the most important point arises when the problem of the sociotechnical reconstruction of the entire society enters into the picture. Kitzinger (1978: 271–72) stresses this point:

> Any reorganization of society which focuses on the needs of women as mothers must involve a re-evaluation of what is important about the mothering role for the community as a whole. Young people growing up should learn that mothers are not second-class citizens, doing a job anyone can do, but individuals who require special skills to perform what is perhaps the most important task for which any human being can prepare themselves, creating the society of the future.

The Private self is the self that one sees exclusively in front of oneself; all secrets, private feelings, and most intimate, shameful, and ego-related experiences remain in the core of this self. Its privacy may be assaulted in many ways and for many reasons. What is private is precious. If one controls something that is private, one is, at the same time, in possession of something of special value. Therefore, not only individuals but also governments (and especially totalitarian ones) use many technical and psychological strategies to enter into the Private self. This gives them opportunities for blackmail. The actual or potential oppression may be twofold here. First, one may use this power to compel somebody to behave in a prescribed way; second, one may use the consequences of the disclosure of the secrets obtained. This disclosure would single out an individual as the target of different types of condemnation. Foucault

(1980) makes the simple observation that, historically, governmental condemnation has shifted its focus from the Real "I" to the Private "I." He says that the study of penal history shows a shift from the repressive, violent forms of governance (mainly corporal and capital punishments) to the milder forms of penance (prisons, enhanced surveillance, inspection, psychological discipline, etc.).

The Private "I," being the element which integrates different selves into a consistent whole, needs an idea as its own central, integrative link. This idea may be generated by the bearer of this self, or it may be taken from outside. There exist enormous numbers of people who are able to develop their own unique and individual selves. It is not only artists, painters, writers, scholars, or political and social leaders who have this particular ability; so-called ordinary people can be very creative in their own private way. They may possess their own sense of identity, their own particular sense of humor, their own understanding of human life, and their own unique and private life goals. As some are unable to generate for themselves their own sense of identity, others may take as their leading ideas those meta-attitudes that have been developed by their mother societies (individual success, task orientation, seniority principle, spectacular principledness, etc.). Even though they are adopted from outside, those ideas may operate as very personal guiding forces. Those who own them are regarded as "characters."

The Private self seems to be tainted by some elements of enigma. Laing goes even further and speaks about the false-self system:

> The false-self system to be described here exists as the complement of an "inner" self which is occupied in maintaining its identity and freedom by being transcendent, unembodied, and thus never grasped, pinpointed, trapped, possessed. Its aim is to be a pure subject, without any objective existence. Thus, except in certain possible safe moments the individual seeks to regard the whole of his objective existence as the expression of a false self (Laing 1969: 94–95).

Therefore, one should regard integrity (in its original sense) as the central axis of the Private "I." The Private "I" prospers as long as it has something that keeps all its diverse elements together. Regarded by some as obsolete, but the only one in existence, Berelson and Steiner's synthesis of 1,045 hypotheses concerning human behavior (which are understood as having varying degrees of probability and accepted with varying degrees of confidence) only marginally mentions the "strain toward consistency" (Berelson and Steiner 1964: 666). This lack of a more developed theoretical synthesis is apparently due to the fact that this remarkable inventory was based on findings describing modern Western man, particularly Americans. Omitted from their work were studies concerning Indians, Arabs, Africans, the peasants of Eastern Europe, the Eastern European intelligentsia, Turkish villagers, eighteenth-century Londoners, and the modern population of Papua New Guinea, medieval knights, Roman slaves, the native peoples of Australia, Canada, and the United States, to name a few omissions. Had these peoples been included in the inventory, its conclusions would surely have corroborated those reached by Ossowska, the founder of the empirical sociology of morality, in her lifelong research.

According to Ossowska's theory of the sociology of morality, moral phenomena have two basic dimensions: the first is utilitarian, and deals with how to deliver pleasures and how to protect from pain those people who belong to a given society; the second is how to live in dignity and secure respect for it (Ossowska 1983: 547–49). If a person loses his/her integrity, he/she is headed toward the destruction of his/her own personality and the uniqueness of his/her self. When his/her integrity is destroyed, his/her personality disintegrates into many diverse elements. The destroyed personality becomes a composite of elements of former education, memories of the past, distaste connected with the feeling that one is in some sense broken, hatred of those who succeeded in imposing their will, impotent dreams of revenge, and the overwhelming impression that one has become alienated even from oneself. On the other hand, those who are able to retain their integrity throughout very difficult periods of their lives still feel that they can keep the rudder in their hands and enter safely into the bay.

Those who have once violated their central integrity (not peripheral integrity, which is connected with certain isolated, nonessential parts of their personality) are inclined to do so again. "Converters" who changed their minds are likely to do it more easily in future. Those who have divorced three times are more likely to do so again than those who have only once. Traitors are not only harmful to those whom they have betrayed; they are most harmful to themselves, for they are destroying their inner compasses and hence are deprived of any sense of direction. Being bad for themselves, they become angry and therefore frustrated. As frustrated people, they become still worse for themselves. Thus, they fall into the trap of their own oppression.

IMPLICATIONS

The first conclusion that emerges from this chapter is that oppression does not come exclusively from outside. As noted earlier, agencies of the criminal justice system such as the police, prisons, or courts may, when abused, oppress people severely (in totalitarian systems, they do so by their very nature). Special, professional practices of agents of social control may be additionally painful. It must be remembered also that there is the quiet oppression that comes from within. The "installing" of an invisible internal agent of social control that is constantly evaluating, judging, monitoring, and possibly punishing one's own behavior exerts a much more subtle, effective, and penetrating control over one's relations with others than even the most sophisticated external measures. Of course, it is necessary to remember that this agent may guide one toward oppression but also toward freedom.

The second conclusion is of a more specific nature; it is a reflection on the use of various forms of pressure that prevail inside of the existing (but historically changeable) criminal justice system. Foucault's well-known central thesis on punishment was summarized in the following way in an interview with J. J. Brochier:

Brochier: You determine one moment as being central in the history of repression: the transition from the inflicting of penalties to the imposition of surveillance.

Foucault: That's correct—the moment where it became understood that it was more efficient and profitable in terms of the economy of power to place people under surveillance than to subject them to some exemplary penalty (Foucault 1980: 38).

This means that it is more effective to attack the very soul (the psyche) than the body of the person who is the subject of social practice. Behind this revealing thesis lies a very simple observation: it is more efficient to shift the target of social control from the concrete body—the Real "I"—to the soul—that is, to the Looking-glass "I," or even to the Private "I." That leads also to an observation that the identification of different levels of selves could be a very fruitful one.

The third conclusion concerns the position of the Private "I" versus other selves. The Private "I" plays the central role in regulating everybody's behavior. Therefore, it could be regarded as the *superself*. The Freudian superego is an unfortunate but suggestive mixture of descriptive and normative elements; it confuses the analysis and description of reality, sociopsychological reality, with ethical requirements—demands of "higher" values, representing the interests of the larger society. The superself, on the contrary, keeps various elements of the psyche together, without introducing into it any evaluative-ethical discriminations. Even a criminal has a superself, since it gives him/her an assurance of the effective operation of his/her whole personality. The superself is not concerned predominantly with moral values, which may be ethically negative or positive. Rather, the superself deals with the task of keeping together the whole psyche (of which positive and negative moral values form a part), by supplying it with the authority of an idea of a higher order.

To successfully construct a sociology of humankind (and thus to depart from the prevailing current practice of developing sociologies of various societies—sociologies of subsystems), one should study in an empirical way different manifestations of superselves as they have been generated in concrete human societies. Such a study could include, for example, the concept of seniority in Japanese society (Nakane 1973); the authoritarian attitude found in German society (Adorno et al. 1950); the spectacular principledness (that is, the approval of certain norms or values because they are considered sacred and symbolically significant) of Polish society (Podgórecki 1979; 1987); or the concept of personal success in American society (Merton 1957). These studies would also indicate that although the Private "I" may have some oppressive characteristics, its major function is the preservation of integrity.

Fourth, it can be concluded that each personality is a composite, more or less stable, of several selves. Some personalities are eclectic assemblies of various selves, whereas others are composed in such a way that certain types of self play dominant roles. A personality that is dominated by the Principled self and that uses the Instrumental, Facade, and some other types of self as its auxiliary components may combine the dignity of the Principled "I" and the adjustment potentialities of the Instrumental and the Facade "I's." The Instrumental "I" which uses the Facade "I" and the Principled "I" (righteous indignation) as its accomplices may serve as an example of the Instrumental "I" (the squared Instrumental "I").

In some situations, especially when an individual faces a vacuum of the self, the Subsidiary self may be readily supplemented by the social control of the totalitarian regime. The Subsidiary self provides the particular person with an adopted self, treated as its own. The Looking-glass "I" may also have far-reaching ethical consequences. If it is understood as an Asian concept of preserving "face," then it easily explains the heavy impact of the phenomenon of "losing face," which is central for Asian ethics. Western ethics, based on the concept of guilt, can be explained as the conflict between the Real self (as it displays itself in reality) and the Ideal self (as demanded from the individual and desired by him or her). The association of the Instrumental self and Real self creates the "basic self." Indeed, under sufficient pressures, an individual may be so stripped of his/her human features as to be left, eventually, with his/her adaptive capabilities and his/her essential needs connected mainly by hunger.

> To pass from civilization to extremity means to be shorn of the elaborate system of relationships—to job, class, tradition and family, to groups and institutions of every kind—which for us provides perhaps ninety percent of what we think we are. In the camps, prisoners lost their possessions,

their social identity, the whole of the cultural matrix which had previously sustained them. They lost, in other words, the delicate web of symbolic identifications available to men and women in normal times. In Nazi camps they lost even their names and their hair (Des Pres 1980: 182).

Fifth, it can be concluded that social groups, small or large, are a mixture of different types of personalities composed of different selves or dominated by certain types of selves. Social groups of revolutionaries would consist mainly of the Principled and Instrumental selves combined with Subsidiary selves; social groups composed of knights would present an almost homogeneous group of individuals based on the Principled and the Facade selves. Social groups of monks would illustrate a nearly homogeneous group of Ideal selves. A proper diagnosis of the global character of the given group provides grounds for predicting its social behavior in the given social circumstances and for determining how a person has to behave if he or she wishes to influence this group's social behavior.

The final conclusion is not directly connected with the main topic. It is that the problem of meta-attitudes is central for reaching the final goal of sociology, whether this is understood to be devising a systematic theory of humankind (organic collections of societies), finding sociotechnical solutions to societal problems, or illuminating the relationship between micro- and macro-. Therefore, it is necessary to stress that the concepts of selves developed in this chapter are not deduced from the very essence of human nature or the hidden intricacies of human psychology. They are treated as the results of different interactions that take place inside various social systems (and subsystems). Social roles that individuals play in various communities shape their internal images, socializing and anchoring those roles in the appropriate "I's" to which they correspond (and which, in some instances, they generate). Thus, the roles design the selves, and the selves determine the roles.

Various attempts have been made to bridge the gap between the micro- and macro- structure and the acting agent. Usually, those who are dealing with the theory of society use very abstract language to cover their inability to establish this link. The reemergence of the concept of differentiated selves presents, among other things, an attempt to see in the microcosm of the individual the complicity of the general social structure, and to see in the societal supraorganization the archetypical patterns embedded in the human "germ" that originated this structure. The concept of different selves not only allows analysis of the same primordial and basic social interhuman network from two opposite perspectives; it also gives the possibility, using various types of selves, of elucidating variations in the different categories of personality and variations in different types of social settings. In other words, it allows us to see specific personalities enriched by their immersion into their society, and to see societies enriched by the interaction of the Pandora's box of humanity.

Without these concepts, it will be impossible to discuss adequately, in empirical and general terms, the attitudes and behaviors of human beings. The cultural development of humankind brings about various types of meta-attitudes. In different societies they are distributed in various ways. Some societies gain a certain type of identity by developing their own combinations of available meta-attitudes, while other societies may forge their identities by creating new types of meta-attitudes and attributing to them the personality-shaping roles. Although there exist various meta-attitudes (selves) that are essential elements of the social systems, there exist, as well, certain leading ideas that are the products of the development of various societies. These ideas may put their own marks on the variety of selves. In effect, human culture is the result of those processes that are generated in the psyche of the human being and those that operate in a larger cultural habitat.

NOTES

1. The concept of meta-attitudes was developed in connection with a series of studies on various moral and legal attitudes of the Polish population. It was elaborated in several of my works published in Poland in the 1970s and, in English, in Podgórecki and Łoś 1979: 159–67. In these studies, a *meta-attitude* was defined as the intermediate, hidden, and invisible factor that sorts and organizes subordinate attitudes into a cohesive whole. This concept was later used (but not quoted) by Marody, who states that her research is focused on "the underlying deeper attitudes toward the social reality of which they [respondents] are not necessarily aware but which do influence their actions within the reality" (Marody 1988: 96).

2. Some authors tend to identify instrumentality with manipulativeness (Christie and Geis 1970), which is not necessarily correct.

3. See also Podgórecki: "True Equality. 'You claim that people are equal,' the emperor Fang said to Si-tien, 'but in reality they may be tall or small, crippled or thin, and so on. What do you have to say to that?' 'People are equal,' insisted Si-tien. 'But people may be wise or stupid, mentally clumsy or innovative or fearful,' Fang went on. 'What is your reply to that?' 'People are equal,' said Si-tien. The emperor began to show signs of irritation. 'But some people are rich, some are upstarts, some are poor, some are princes, some are beggars, and few are like you. How can that be? In what way are they equal—tell me!' 'In vanity, self-love, and envy,' replied Si-tien" (A. Podgórecki, *The Thoughts of Si-tien*, London: Poets and Painters Press, 1988).

4. The concealed self is to be regarded as a sub-category of the Facade self. The concealed self does not want to reveal its real identity and its most inherent values. It hides what is most important to it, as though it were an exclusively treasured secret. Although the concealed self constantly presents itself as some-

thing else, it does not want to lose its true identity; unlike the Facade self that has a more or less visible tendency to identify itself with its own visionary image. The concealed self does not have the slightest intention of condemning or rejecting its own true character. At the same time, the concealed self sits in two different chairs.

There are many reasons why an individual may sustain (or may be compelled to sustain) this "double-life" strategy. Usually, it is the result of an overwhelming pressure to conform, a pressure of survival. The causes of this strategy can be social, biological, psychological or cognitive. They can be connected with an attachment to two cultures: (a) double religions, (b) national or cultural identity, (c) deviant (or regarded as deviant) biological conditioning, (d) events that forcibly split the genuine, personal identity, (e) conscious, cognitive determination of an ideological or pragmatical character (for example, double-agent's psyche).

Although these various determinations are interesting subjects of an independent inquiry, the consequences of this type of life-strategy are, at present, more significant. This strategy forces an individual into a state of constant alertness, with an instrumental readiness to compare, match, relate, evaluate, choose, decide, re-decide, make perpetual corrections, retrieve, obliterate tracks, give misleading signals, and invent new ways to hide. Obviously, these pressures tend to sometimes stimulate the concealed self toward inventiveness, originality, intellectual creativity, or artistic ingenuity, but they mainly impel the self toward maneuvering, manipulation, and actions based on ploy. Thus, the concealed "hidden agenda" self can be regarded as one of the most influential sources of social development and maneuverability.

In sum, all these small strategies of survival systematically reinforce the simultaneous maintenance and cultivation of two different self-identities, which reveal only one identity to the outside social world.

5. The "workers' courts" were set up in accordance with the policy generally adopted in the East Bloc under the regime of Communism.

6. Personal communication from Arnold M. Rose.

3

Behavior Under Oppression

Camus's novel *The Plague* (1977, first published in 1947) describes an imaginary society in a large city that is attacked by a deadly epidemic. In the course of the story, one may distinguish fifteen stages in the advancement and withdrawal of oppression. The first is the stage of everyday normalcy. The second is characterized by the emergence of various types of new and unrecognized symptoms (strange circumstances, calling for an alarm, inducing a tendency to ignore them, etc.). The third stage heralds the social recognition that the newly emerged symptoms constitute a common danger. The fourth consists of attempts to fight against the puzzling but deadly danger with measures that traditionally were regarded as useful in battling various calamities. The fifth stage is marked by a growing social presentiment of an approaching general crisis, and the sixth, by a socially shared feeling of despair: Why did it happen to me? Why did it happen to us?

The seventh stage of oppression consists of various types of social reactions toward the catastrophe, whether withdrawal, animated religious activity, real or spurious indifference, overt or hidden anger, irrational behavior, engagement with a second ("shadow") economy, open refusal to adapt, excessive optimism, or various sorts of social pathology. The eighth stage is typified by its clear image of collective identity: "We oppressed." This stage constitutes the peak of the crisis.

In the ninth stage comes the first hope of relief; to some extent, those hopes are justified by new technical and organizational inventions in the war with the plague. The tenth stage sees a far-reaching cry for a "new social order," at which point the plague turns itself into its own opposition. The eleventh stage is an acute, painful feeling that rescue is still not close enough. The twelfth is the first massive withdrawal of the calamity; the thirteenth, a recurrent wave of pain. A general return to "normalcy" comes with stage fourteen, which marks the closing of the circle. In the fifteenth and the final stage comes the awareness that the evil that was defeated has merely returned to its dormant form.

Translated thus into sociological language, *The Plague* presents abundant and suggestive material for the development of a synthetic model of macrosocial oppression (imaginative and insightful penetration of social reality is often much more illuminating than laborious and dull sociological inquiries). This chapter outlines at the microlevel descriptions of human behaviors that arise in situations of man-made oppression. It does so through a series of hypotheses about features of behavior under oppression that are specific to various types of social situations. These hypotheses provide general frameworks for human behavior; different types of selves modify this behavior, but they do it inside of those already predesigned skeletons.

According to Merton, the dominant mode of behavior in nonoppressive situations is conformist. Conformity, he says,

> is the most common and widely diffused [type of adaptation]. Were this not so, the stability and continuity of the society could not be maintained. The mesh of expectancies constituting every social order is sustained by the modal behaviour of its members representing conformity to be established, though perhaps secularly changing, culture patterns (Merton 1968: 195).

The thrust of the hypotheses that follow is that in oppressive situations, conformity as such ceases to be the dominant mode of adaptive behavior. Although the hypotheses are formulated in a typically positivist manner, it must be noted that they are not exclusively concerned with objective data taken from outside; that is, with the data that are given, that can be measured, standardized, and translated into testable statements. Instead, the hypotheses are concerned with subjective constructions, developed by the agents of human interaction. These constructions can have objective counterparts, but they may also represent only pure products of human minds, emotions, and myths. Human interactions can, by visible activities, change social reality or communications and involve people in task-oriented activities, but they may also capture and oppress individuals by meanings that individuals themselves attribute to them, all because human beings can be seized by their own imaginations.

HYPOTHESIS ONE

Berelson and Steiner list the features that have been identified by several studies as belonging to the authoritarian personality. These features may be regarded as one of the main predispositions to oppressive behavior.

> Thus according to them, the studies found that the following traits designated "authoritarianism" tend to occur in combination: great concern with authority, involving deference to superiors and assertiveness towards underlings; little personal regard for others; a tendency to "manipulate and exploit" and the expectation of being similarly treated; conventionality, conformity, lack of "individuality"; strict "morality," self-righteousness, moral indignation; failure to accept one's own "immoral" impulses coupled with the tendency to attribute evil intent and actions to other groups, particularly minorities; stereotyped, inflexible "black-and-white" thinking; intolerance, bigotry, superstition; general hostility, destructiveness, cynicism; exaggerated concern with sex (Berelson and Steiner 1964: 259).

Thus, one of the most important features of the authoritarian personality is a preoccupation with the phenomenon of authority. If someone is unable to escape the overwhelming pressure of authority, he or she may desert into the realm of false consciousness. Once on this track, he/she may identify himself/herself with the oppressor. This peculiar escape route gives him several real advantages. The first is that, since he/she is now an oppressor himself/herself, he/she is "mighty" and does not have to be afraid. The second is that as an oppressor, he/she has a feeling of immunity against possible aggression. And the third is that this type of security gives him/her a reassuring feeling of belonging to the world of the powerful, the world that decides the fates of others, including the very fate that was his/hers before his/her transmutation. According to Fromm (1942: 121):

> The first mechanism of escape I am going to deal with is the tendency to give up the independence of one's own individual self and to fuse one's self with somebody or something outside ourselves in order to acquire the strength which the individual self is lacking. Or, to put it in different words, to seek for new, "secondary bonds" as a substitute for the primary bonds which have been lost.

The only weak point of this defense strategy is that the *real* oppressor does not know anything about this transmutation and will therefore not exempt its subject from oppressive treatment. One of the essential elements of the authoritarian personality is the attitude toward receiving and giving orders.

HYPOTHESIS TWO

People have a tendency to obey orders that come from authorities they accept, regardless of the content of the orders. Some social experiments shed an intriguing light on the phenomenon of obedience and, consequently, oppression. The Milgram experiment suggests that human beings have a tendency to exert unusually strong pressure on others when they act as agents carrying out orders from a legitimate power (Milgram 1974: 35). Miller (1986: 9) summarized Milgram's findings in the following way:

> Forty subjects participated in the experiment described in the 1963 publication (Milgram 1974). Of these, 26 pressed the 450-volt switch. This resulted in an obedience rate of 65 percent—which is the major finding of the study. It has become, certainly, the best known result of the entire obedience research project despite the fact that in a number of Milgram's experiments the obedience rate dropped to zero. Thus, the 65 percent obedience result has become, in effect, a baseline finding against which other findings, including people's intuitive perception, are compared.

Indeed, the findings of this experiment are shocking. A series of parallel experiments substantially documented a general statement according to which human beings comply, almost uncritically, with orders coming from "above." Follow-up inquiries conducted around the world, in Germany, Australia, and Jordan, support these findings as well (see Miller 1986: 68, 71, 75).

Although these conclusions have been discussed from many possible angles, including, if not predominantly, the ethical appropriateness of research of this type, the question why people are so obedient was not sufficiently elucidated. The idea of agency (acting as someone's delegate) seems to be a weak point of the empirical and conceptual scheme developed by Milgram. An alternative explanation proposes itself. During the ongoing socialization process, individuals in all possible settings (family, school, workplace, church, community, political party, etc.) are constantly exposed to various commands from higher ranks. This exposure to different categories of charges generates a general blanket readiness to behave in a required way. Thus, this readiness is not only conditioned by numerous previous commands but also by the observation that those commands are, as a rule, guided by a high degree of technical rationality and, quite often, by a tendency to observe the common good (the meaning of which is tailored to the interests of those who are in charge). Therefore, any command given by an authority with power at its disposal sets into motion a *dormant, accumulated and prearranged potential*. This potential of motivation constitutes a dispositional pool of action that may be put into behavioral reality without delay.

Needless to say, this readiness to fulfill actual commands and the willingness to obey could be used, sometimes without ethical limitations, to introduce, reinforce, and execute various types of oppression. It is interesting to note that people, as a rule, are incognizant of their inner potentials. Before his research on obedience, Milgram asked 110 subjects from various groups (psychiatrists, college students, middle-class adults) about their own imagined behavior as the executors of received orders. "They believed that only a small, pathological fringe of about one in a thousand people would go as far as the maximum shock level" (Gerbing and Buskist 1990: 620).

The Zimbardo experiment was enlightening as well. In 1972 Zimbardo and his colleagues conducted an experiment at Stanford University that consisted of creating a make-believe prison. Theatrical accessories were used to lend it an air of reality, and the artificial prison allowed for observation of its occupants. Twenty-two young people were selected from those who responded to a newspaper advertisement and were divided randomly into two categories: guards and prisoners. Neither guards nor prisoners were instructed on how to behave in these new circumstances. Immediately, both groups split into two strictly separate populations. The guards as well as the prisoners rushed into their assigned roles with such zeal that they almost instantly lost all sense of the artificial character of the experiment. Contrary to the original intention, the experiment was completed in six days instead of the planned two weeks because of the prisoners' violently growing dissatisfaction, depression, attempts to escape, and so on.

The results of this experiment clearly showed that it was not the "oppressor mentality," the negative preselection (inducing those people who had a wish to volunteer in order to oppress others), nor the negative prisoners' subculture that was responsible for the development of the atmosphere of oppression. Rather there were certain features specific to institutions, certain types of social organizations and elements inherent in the structure, some unique internal processes, and apparently some images adopted from the mass media that induced negative social behavior. Thus, it is possible to conclude that social constructs like institutions, organizations, and legal structures start to function as independent variables (causes) and may, contrary to their goals, start to operate as instruments and tools of unanticipated oppression.

Both the Milgram and the Zimbardo experiments provide some additional data for understanding human conduct. In each case, it is the experimental method that makes it possible to eliminate certain factors and to accentuate others. Both experiments show that people may oppress themselves not only more or less directly and intentionally but also through the use of social artifices that are created as "socially neutral" devices.

HYPOTHESIS THREE

Under the stress of oppression, either perceived as objective or even subjectively generated, an individual has three options. One is to withdraw from social life and its activities, to become socially "invisible." The second is to engage in hyperconformist social interactions, to become "lost inside the human crowd." The third is to go "underground."

The first option could be called an escape into marginality. Generating from his empirical research based on the analysis of about 700 autobiographies, Znaniecki divided people into four categories. To one category belonged those who were "well-bred"; those who received a respectable *Kinder-Stube* (proper family upbringing) as an introduction to adult life and who, therefore, tended to respect strictly all the requirements of proper social manners. To the second category belonged those who were engaged in constant play; they regarded life as one great opportunity for their own pleasure and excitement. The third category consisted of those who were, from early childhood, socialized to manual or mental work; in short, those who were socialized to be task-oriented. To the fourth category belonged those who were "deviant"; this category was subdivided into "especially gifted" and "marginal," including criminals (Znaniecki 1934).

Using Znaniecki's classification as a framework, one may hypothesize that in an oppressive situation, the number of those who belong to the marginal-deviant subcategory would increase dramatically. Indeed, unusual psychological and social pressures would force people to behave in ways that departed from generally accepted standards. People would tend to find various small ways to deal with the steadily mounting pressures and with the unexpected complications of social reality. They would, in effect, create a special social stratum of marginals who might manifest their existence by means of highly developed corruption or a bohemian style of life. This stratum would be characterized by strange, diversified values, unconventional ethoses, unexpected life experiences and a variety of incompatible *Weltanschauung*, or worldviews. This group might create a highly developed, illegal but functional "second economy" (Łoś 1990). It would not only sanction many peculiar life-styles but would also actively absorb into its marginalized center many of those on the periphery.

The second option, transformation into a hyperconformistic ethos, has clear functionalist entanglements. As the number of distinctive elements within the amorphous masses grows, there are more and more opportunities for hiding within the "lonely" and "one-dimensional" crowd. That is, individuals who are, from one point of view, increasingly marginalized and diversified become, paradoxically enough, from another point of view, more and more alike. They dress in a similar way, they behave in a similar fashion, they arrange their houses in a similar style, they gesticulate in the same manner; they even enjoy using exactly the same gestures, words, pet names, or love whispers. One should understand hyperconformist behavior as behavior that does not restrict conformity to means alone (ritualistic behavior) but that is strictly conformist as far as goals are concerned as well. It is not overly conformist behavior, which may represent deviancy or overt conformity (Merton 1968: 236), nor is it zealous neophytic behavior. Rather, hyperconformist behavior treats prescribed norms of behavior as fixed and strictly autotelic values, values for themselves.

The third option of individual response under oppression is hardly recognized in modern sociology. This is the life of a secret organization. With the exception of Simmel (1950) and especially Aubert (1965), whose work is based primarily upon his reminiscences of participation in a secret intelligence organization during the German occupation of Norway in World War II, human relations, as they are shaped by the imposition of an outside dominance and kept under secrecy, have not been sufficiently analyzed. This is puzzling: why is the strategy of oppression so well elaborated from the point of view of its designers but neglected from the point of view of the victims who have been actively fighting the oppressors?

Aubert's main thesis is that "secrecy is the basic weapon of the underground—above everything else, secrecy about the borderlines of the organization, about who is a member and who is not" (Aubert 1965: 289). Thus, occupation creates two worlds: an official world, whose existence is shaped by the imposed power (with elements like compulsory work; mistrust of public institutions; systematic extortion and plunder of private goods; life in a "void"; myths; corruption; rapid development of social pathology; and decreasing influence of social control) and an unofficial world, whose existence is influenced by close informal ties (a strict division between "we" and "they"; mutual help based on family and friendship ties; a feeling of the omnipresent existence of the secretive underground army; faith in the future; an atmosphere of patriotic sacrifice; contempt for the invaders).

There are many interesting phenomena connected with struggle to survive collectively and individually during a period of oppression. One of the most characteristic seems to be a strong yearning for legend, or *myth*. Various collective and individual myths screen the otherwise carefully hidden activities of those who escaped underground. Also important is the power of *inertia*, which is so highly visible when oppression is finally removed. One can outlive the period of oppression, but certain habits, small ways of behavior, peculiar types of adjustment (including "secondary adjustment," see page 49), and unique patterns of human relations may stick with victims even if the cause has totally disappeared. Legends created during the period of underground activity may be regarded by some as the most important parts of their lives. Thus, behavior under oppression tends to perpetuate its own patterns of action even when the oppression has been successfully abolished.

HYPOTHESIS FOUR

Under oppression, the General self, that self that encompasses all other existing selves, shrinks to a combination of the Real self and the Instrumental self. What does this mean? In a brutal, crushing, oppressive situation when one's very survival is at stake, a human being is unable to elaborate and build various masks; to observe others carefully in order to figure out what they think about him or her; to speculate how far he or she is from the ideal which he or she regards as his/her own "polar star"; to stick to binding principles (categorical imperatives) independent of obstacles of surrounding circumstances; to contemplate inner thoughts and feelings; or to identify himself/herself with the values of others. In this situation a human being fights for life.

To face this fight, a human being must respect the demands of his/her Real self, the self that consists of all material and physiological determinants that influence the life of an individual. Sometimes the demands of the Real self are quite heavy. The reality of the concentration camp may serve as an example.

> In history and in life one sometimes seems to glimpse a ferocious law which states: "To he that has, will be given; to he that has not, will be taken away." In the *Lager* (German term for concentration camp), where man is alone and where the struggle for life is reduced to its primordial mechanism, this unjust law is openly in force, is recognized by all (Levi 1961: 80).

To survive, however, a human being must also employ any accessible means and tools which his/her Instrumental self may find useful—the Instrumental self being that which is disposed to suspend the spontaneous reaction to given social stimuli; to calculate possible losses and gains through analysis of various strategic options; to act according to a subjective vision of individual interests; and to accommodate itself to the existing state of affairs. Otherwise put, to cite an observation drawn from the same concentration camp:

> One needed an intelligence that was nondogmatic; that reacted flexibly to the environment, drawing the most apt conclusions from a concrete situation over which one had no control. Only such an attitude and skill enabled one to make a relevant moral choice (Pawelczynska 1979: 140).

In such a situation, the General self takes with it to the battleground only two selves, those that are best equipped to undertake the fight for survival: they are the Real and Instrumental selves.

HYPOTHESIS FIVE

Thus, the Individual self engaged in the task of defending its very existence develops various personal strategies of protection. Nonetheless, an individual living in a web of social interrelations also becomes engaged in the additional task of creating complicated sets of interpersonal social relations of a defensive character. Canadian-born Goffman calls these social relations a "secondary adjustment" and says they consist of "any habitual arrangement by which a member of an organization employs unauthorized means, or obtains unauthorized ends, or both, thus getting around the organization's assumptions as to what he should do and get and hence what he should be" (Goffman 1961: 189).

An individual under the pressure of imposed conformist behavior, which, with all its mutual agreements and obligations, is still too heavy for his/her shoulders, may conclude that the only reasonable way to shed this unbearable burden is to throw it on somebody else's back. Since legal rules may not allow such behavior, the individual in question is pushed to act against the law. In this way, behaviors under oppression are directly linked with extralegal or antilegal activities. Thus, whereas in nonoppressive situations, human behavior is mainly regulated by primary adjustment—adapting to existing circumstances under the guidance of the accepted conventions—in oppressive situations secondary adjustment appears to be the rule.

This concept was expressed by Reinaldo Arenas (1989: 68) in his captivating prose: "Arturo realized, saw, that indifference was a deadly foe to them (and to the others and the rest and everyone else, for that matter), that is, that vulgarity, imbecility, horror, would not suffer indifference; treason, robbery, insult, murder, you could do anything, and many did, but what you could not do, what was absolutely not allowed, was at the moment of committing the crime (both before and after) to underestimate the immense vulgarity, not take it into account, not to submit to it, become part of it . . . no, if you wanted to survive you had to adapt or fake adaptation."

HYPOTHESIS SIX

In oppressive situations, mutual social empathy (such as might arise between oppressors and oppressed, and among the oppressed themselves) is quite often purposefully reduced to a minimum. The reduction of empathy engineered by the oppressors takes place mainly for pragmatic reasons: in order to facilitate the undertaking, continuing, and finishing of their tasks. Modern "total institutions," in order to handle a considerable number of inmates, employ various processes of segregation, unification, and technical labelling. Many of these processes have distinctive features of mortification of the oppressed individual. Thus, "upon entrance, he is immediately stripped by these [social] arrangements. In the accurate language of some of our oldest total institutions, he begins a series of abasements, degradations, humiliations, and profanations of self. His self is systematically, if often unintentionally, mortified" (Goffman 1961: 14). Sometimes, these processes are brought into play for criminal reasons. Steiner (1969: 78) gives an example:

> Months passed before the legendary Eureka! was heard. It was Becker who uttered it. He devised a van in which the exhaust pipe fed into the interior of the back part, which was hermetically sealed. The victims were killed by carbon monoxide. Becker, who did experiments before sending the plan through official channels, had calculated by observing a certain ratio between the cylinder capacity of the motor of the van and the volume of the sealed chamber in which the victims were imprisoned, the latter should die peacefully by going to sleep within ten to fifteen minutes, given the motor running at moderate speed. Consequently, he suggested that ditches be dug about ten miles from the points of concentration of the Jews, which would allow the vans, driving twenty-five miles an hour, to reach them with a security margin of five to ten minutes. The "technicians" (German planners)[1] were immediately attracted by the simplicity and rationality of the plan.

In this case, the "technicians" were involved in their own task-oriented activities. Nonetheless they were quite eager to trigger some semispontaneous processes by which they could distract the oppressed, imposing on them absorbing tasks that would keep them from engaging in any resistance activities or mutual-help arrangements.

It was an old "technician's" principle to make the Jews believe that work equalled life. It was one of their first arguments at the time of the ghetto. ... The "technicians" said, "Work and your life will be spared." The Jews thought, "They need our labour, so they will let us live." This was a mistake, of course, and the "technicians" gained on two grounds: in the first place the Jews worked for them, and in the second place this work, which they saw as security, disarmed them morally and psychologically (Steiner 1969: 361–62).

These tactics were a logical consequence of a more general and vicious strategy: Making the victims the accomplices of their own executioners was a kind of dogma to the "technicians." It was for the sake of this principle that they had made Vilna [ghetto in Vilna] destroy itself, and it must be admitted that the results had been more than satisfying (Steiner 1969: 100).

In effect, the oppressed were so preoccupied with their own individual defense tactics that they were unable to prepare a common defense strategy. Being successfully atomized, they lost almost all interhuman attachments and became suspicious (maybe somebody else has a better survival strategy? maybe somebody else wants to steal my own defense techniques? maybe somebody else is a dangerous informer? maybe somebody else exploits my defense resources?). Thus they lost the ability to present an integrated front of resistance.

Not only technicians dealing with technique were "efficient"; those who were occupied with organizational problems were "businesslike" as well.

Payment [transportation to the extermination camp] had to be made for only one way. The guards, of course, had to have return fare paid for them because they were going back to their place of origin.

Excuse me, the children under four who were shipped to the extermination camps, the children under four ... went free.

They had the privilege to be gassed freely?

Yes, transport was free (Lanzmann 1985: 142).

It is interesting to note that the idea of "technicians" was later taken up by Lanzmann as the basic concept in the movie and in the book *Shoah*. It is also interesting that neither Lanzmann nor Simone de Beauvoir, who wrote the introductions to both the Steiner and Lanzmann books, mentions this interrelation. But, in the case of Lanzmann, Simone de Beauvoir (in Lanzmann 1985: ix) writes:

One of Claude Lanzmann's great skills has in fact been to tell us the story of the Holocaust from its victim's viewpoint, as well as from that of the "technicians" who made it possible but reject all responsibility for it. One of the most typical is the bureaucrat who organizes the transport. He explains that special trains were made available to holiday or excursion groups at half-fare. He does not deny that the trains sent to the camps were also special trains, but claims he did not know that the camps meant extermination.

Sometimes even the sense of empathy among fellow inmates was successfully eliminated. Piekarski (1989: 251) gives a succinct description of this process:

> From my first day in Auschwitz, I was conditioned to behave—instinctively behave—like a hunted animal. I avoided predators by hiding in the "middle of the herd," thus exposing those around me to immediate danger. I became insensitive to human misery and looked with indifference on the fate of my colleagues. I was not in the position of predator myself, but witnessing remorseless killings by SS men and kapos, I no longer made judgements about who was a "good" man and who was a "bad" man.

The elimination of empathy also takes place in modern terrorist subcultures. Professional terrorists are socialized by their "masters" in a way designed to deprive them of any empathetic feeling. Bakunin's catechism (also known as Nachaeyeff's "Revolutionary Catechism") formulates the following recommendations for an adept terrorist:

> Tyrannical toward himself, he must be tyrannical toward others. All the soft and tender affections arising from kinship, friendship, and love, all gratitude even all honour must be obliterated, and in their place there must be the cold and single-minded passion for the work of revolution. . . . The nature of the true revolutionary excludes all romanticism, all sensitivity, all exaltations and enthusiasm. . . . When a comrade is caught in a dangerous extremity and the question arises whether he should be rescued or not rescued, the revolutionary must make his decision without recourse to personal feelings, but only in terms of the eventual success of the revolution (Rapoport 1979: 80–81).

According to these principles of socialization, terrorists are not only deprived of their own private selves but also, in order to fill up the resulting vacuum, thus receive a package of abstract and cognitive precepts on how to realize an illusory utopia.

HYPOTHESIS SEVEN

Oppression generates frustration; frustration builds aggression; aggression may be directed against oneself or against others. Oppression may be direct, indirect, manifest, or suppressed. The most penetrating psychological study in areas closely connected with social oppression was an inquiry conducted by Grygier (1954 and 1973). His research focused on social and personality changes under different levels of oppression. As related by the author in one of his lectures at Carleton University in 1990, he gained insight into some problems associated with oppressive conditions of deportation and labor camps when he was a prisoner in a labor camp in the former Soviet Union. Instead of regarding himself as an unfortunate victim of injustice, Grygier adopted the detached attitude of the social scientist and seized the opportunity to become a participant observer in the forbidden zone that he had involuntarily penetrated; he started planning his study and the book while in the camp.

Later, Grygier conducted scientifically controlled and statistically tested research based on displaced persons and former inmates of concentration camps. He collected his data in Germany in 1946; all of his subjects were Polish. He examined the personal data of some 5,000 people, tested and interviewed 752 of them, and selected 152 for the final comparison of groups matched in terms of sex, age, education, intelligence, occupation, and region of resistance. Grygier found no relationship between these factors and their bearers' social adjustment or direction of aggression as revealed by personality tests.

The most important findings were concerned with the direction of aggression, demonstrated by the rate of criminality after liberation, which was found to be forty-five times higher in the most oppressed group than in the less-oppressed control group. Psychological tests showed that the higher the level of oppression had been, the greater the subsequent tendency toward "extrapunitive" responses on Rosenzweig's Picture-Frustration Study (PFS). The test measures personality at the level of action. Oppressed subjects tended to (1) blame and accuse others, instead of admitting guilt or stating that nobody was to blame; (2) insist that others should serve them by fulfilling their needs (i.e., they felt in general that the world owed them a living) instead of being optimistic or willing to take responsibility for themselves; or (3) show rigidity and egocentricity in their responses.

The results of Murray's Thematic Apperception Test (TAT) showed that, at a deeper level, the oppressed subjects saw themselves as nonaggressive, innocent victims; it was the world around them that was hostile, oppressive, and aggressive. Both results were confirmed when Grygier tested a small group of Polish Jews, the most oppressed group in the entire study. In this group, all subjects strongly denied any guilt, but at the deeper level harbored devastating guilt feelings. Interviews showed that the subjects felt guilty for surviving when all other members of their families had been sent to the gas chambers. Grygier concludes his inquiry (1973: 286) with an idea that "identification with the aggressor" leads oppressed groups to become oppressors when the opportunity arises. They continue to see themselves as innocent victims in a hostile world and react to the new situation by blaming others and making demands on them. Their guilt feelings become suppressed and blame denied. On the other hand, if an oppressed person can remain tolerant by trying to understand his oppressors, he may feel less need to persecute them.

HYPOTHESIS EIGHT

In some extreme instances, those living under oppression may develop special ties that strengthen the values of human solidarity. These mutual bonds of reinforcement may provide the oppressed with a sense of existence, support them with attitudes of personal dignity, and tie them to values that intrude upon the boundaries of their captivity (patriotic, religious, or ideological values). These mutual reinforcements may supply them with a psychical strength that can replace their disappearing physical strength. In such an extreme situation, oppression may lead to rebellion. Merton (1968: 210) discusses the phenomenon of rebellion in legitimized settings, but his generalizations could be *mutatis mutandis* transferred to an illegitimate social framework:

> When the institutional system is regarded as the barrier to the satisfaction of legitimized goals, the stage is set for rebellion as an adaptive response. To pass into organized political action, allegiance must not be withdrawn from the prevailing political structure but must be transferred to new groups possessed of a new myth.

Thus, one could say that when the pain of surviving in a nonlegitimized institutional system outweighs the drive to survive, then rebellion could occur. Moreover, it could occur even if (1) the rebels never felt allegiance to the system; (2) the existing system never created a myth justifying itself; and, in extraordinary conditions, (3) the rebellion has no chance of success. Under such circumstances, the rebellion would be only a heroic, dramatic gesture by which the oppressed could rise from their humiliation and regain their dignity. This type of rebellion might be called a "self-ennobling ceremony" as opposed to a "degradation ceremony" (Garfinkel 1965: 420–24).

Enriched access to information may also play an important role in the perception of oppression and in the establishment of solidarity against it. This situation became especially clear in Aubert's insightful analysis (1965: 297) based on his "participant observation" of Norwegian underground activities during World War II:

> Although their [the members of the underground] inside information was pitifully inadequate, it did put them in a relatively less deprived position

with respect to information than the majority of the population. Since relative deprivation and relative privilege may often be more psychologically meaningful than the absolute magnitudes of privilege and deprivation, this slightly superior access to knowledge made one feel less oppressed and more in command of one's fate.

HYPOTHESIS NINE

An acute social crisis is apt to generate a charismatic figure. If such a figure is on the horizon, it is easy to guess that a critical social conflict is under way. These two phenomena are interlinked. The charismatic figure could be of the positive type (for example, Joan of Arc, Mohandas Gandhi, Martin Luther King, or Lech Walesa) or of a negative sort (Stalin, Hitler, Jim Jones or David Koresh). What is important is that, when rational rules of social conduct are in question and when rationality itself is in doubt, there emerges a widespread need to invoke a hero who, due to his/her superhuman qualities, would be able to solve the problems at hand. The charismatic leader may impose his/her abilities on the masses, who are expecting him/her to do so, or the masses can label someone a leader even before he/she feels any desire to be one. But the charismatic leader always personifies a myth, a dream that is around the corner. In the presidential race in Poland in December 1990, an absolute unknown, Stan Tyminski, emerged as a central figure toward the end of the campaign. Tyminski momentarily became a charismatic phenomenon for three closely linked reasons: (1) he was Canadian, and in Poland the very word *Canada* is synonymous with success; (2) he was a millionaire, meaning he knew how to achieve success and, as president, he would be able to disseminate this knowledge; and finally (3) in a situation where austerity was desperately needed, and in a situation where the socioeconomic crisis created by the Marxist government was acute, a promise of immediate economic success would be a self-promoting mechanism of enormous force.

There exist "large" charismatic figures (Churchill, Wilson, Stalin, Hitler) and "small" (Bethune, Mother Theresa, Jones, Tyminski). In either case, there remains one stable feature of extraordinary quality.

Weber always used the term "charisma" in the sense of the "extraordinary quality," possessed by persons or objects, that is thought to give these persons or objects a unique, magical power. In his analysis of domination, the term designated one of his three major types. The man who possesses genuine charisma exercises domination, but his power of command differs from legal and traditional domination in that it is extraordinary (Bendix 1977: 299).

There are many types of achievements—and only a few of them have a charismatic character—that lead to the securing of domination. Almost all of them contain some elements of oppression. A court case in 1990 in the former Soviet Union provides a painful but picturesque example of the deeper meaning of domination as exercised at a low level of the army's hierarchy. The case concerns a soldier who was socialized to the informal position that he was supposed to occupy:

> In a deeper sense the State vs. Zvezdin offered a parable of life in the Soviet military, an illuminating glimpse of the forces ripping apart the world's largest army—and the country as well. In courtroom No. 1 on Sept. 24, it was possible to understand why several thousand conscripts— including 430 young Uzbeck men—died or committed suicide last year; why the Soviet armed forces as a beneficent melting pot is a lie; why the centrifugal tugs of *dedovshichina* (*dedovshichina*—the brutal, pervasive and often racist hazing of junior conscripts by senior conscripts) and draft dodging will help compel a radical overhaul of the Soviet army, recalcitrant generals notwithstanding (Atkinson and Lee 1990: 19).

These constant, invisible, pressures may, in some instances, transform themselves into charismatic domination, particularly if the imposter is skillful enough to add to his/her sheer force some persuasive elements of personal charm along with some ideological justifications.

The reverse may also be true. Real charismatic domination may degenerate into sheer oppression when personal and individual virtues disappear, are unmasked, inflated, or found to be nonexistent. In the present world, there are many examples of "fiefdoms" working vigorously to reinforce their positions within already established administrative and bureaucratic structures. These more or less charismatic fiefdoms may operate in universities, research institutes, the army, various branches of bureaucracy, and hospitals, and may also manifest themselves in conventional and aberrant religious groups. Sometimes they can oppress individuals almost as effectively as totalitarian regimes do.

HYPOTHESIS TEN

During oppression, and especially after a period of prolonged oppression, those who have been oppressed conceive their own defense philosophy founded on a need to explain their survival. This happens because oppression, as a rule, actively implicates the oppressed into its world. During the first period of the Stalinist imposition of a "socialist" regime in Poland, I knew a Polish patriot who was adamant about not undertaking any possible work. According to him, any kind of job would contribute, more or less directly, to the entrenchment of the regime imposed by the Soviets. After a time, a group of his friends and students decided to collect among themselves some monthly funds to enable him and his wife to survive. Although their noble gesture did indeed allow this patriot to keep his hands clean, it also meant that those who contributed to his survival had to dirty their own hands.

Those who survived concentration camps, both German and Soviet, repeatedly claim that the strongest imperative behind their endurance and survival was the need to "give testimony," and that this imperative kept them alive.

> Rejected by mankind, the condemned do not go so far as to reject it in turn. Their faith in history remains unshaken, and one may wonder why. They do not despair. The proof: they persist in surviving—not only to survive, but to testify. The victims elect to become witnesses (Wiesel 1972).

One should remember, however, Pareto's deep methodological recommendation: people usually present certain types of facades, or masks, for the outside world and keep to themselves the true, hidden motives of their own behavior.

> The schemer consciously aims at *m* and preaches *T*; but the same thing is done by many individuals in all good faith. Cynically selfish people are rare, and downright hypocrites equally so. The majority of men and women merely desire to reconcile their own advantage with the residues of sociality; realize their own happiness while seeming to strive for the happiness of others; cloak their self-seeking under mantles of religion, ethics, patriotism, humanitarianism, party loyalty, and so on; work for material satisfaction while seeming to be working only for ideals (Pareto 1983, section 1884).

It is necessary to remember that in a situation of accumulated oppression it would be enormously difficult to establish which motives were authentic. Additionally, some derivations (justifications, rationalizations) that in the beginning appear only as a cover may, after many repetitions on various occasions and after certain memories have been persistently pushed out of mind, appear to their proponents first as probable, later as real, and eventually as true and totally genuine.

CONCLUSIONS

The foregoing considerations of behavior under to man-made oppression suggest the following conclusions.

First, oppression varies in its type, degree of persistence, and acuteness. Sometimes it consists of more than the joking suggestions of peers who exercise their own social-control type of censorship, but sometimes it takes the form of physical torture. The results of extreme oppression are described by Nyiszli (1977: 48–49) in an understated manner:

> The bodies were not lying here and there throughout the room, but piled in mass to the ceiling. The reason for this was that the gas first inundated the lower layers of air and rose but slowly towards the ceiling. This forced the victims to trample one another in a frantic effort to escape the gas. Yet a few feet higher up the gas reached them. What a struggle for life there must have been! Nevertheless it was merely a matter of two or three minutes' respite. If they had been able to think about what they are doing, they would have realized they are trampling their own children, their wives, their relatives. But they couldn't think. Their gestures were not more than reflexes of the instinct of self-preservation. I noticed that the bodies, which were covered with scratches and bruises from the bodies of the women, the children, and the aged were at the bottom of the pile; at the top, the strongest.

Secondly, social interactions taking place under oppressive regimes differ substantially from interactions that are not influenced by oppression. Those not influenced by oppression are characterized mainly by activities of a conformist or ritualist nature (which manifest themselves especially in continuous, repetitive, everyday life behavior), whereas the former are characterized by activities of an instrumental ("secondary adjustment"), withdrawing (hyperconformistic) or rebellious nature, evidently belong to the margin of ordinary human behavior. The apparent domination of conformist behavior in nonoppressive life could be explained by the fact that this type of behavior is demanded by informal and formal social-control apparatuses operating in any social system to achieve goals of the system. Since the existing social-control apparatus has several aims (such as keeping the social system far from overt social conflicts; keeping under control behaviors connected with the griefs of acute social problems; and keeping the social system far from various types of social deviancy), then this apparatus tends to mold collective and individual behavior in a way that matches these goals.

Social interactions under pressure provide a different picture. Activities of withdrawal or those of an innovative (instrumental) character obviously dominate. The preponderance of these activities is determined by the threat to their very existence, by the problem of survival for each individual. Consequently, this picture of human activity has an anatomy of an entirely different type. The specific type of conformist behavior referred to here as hyperconformity is not, in fact, a form of compliance with the dominant values and norms, but a covert strategy of withdrawal (how to hide, how to camouflage oneself behind the shoulders of the co-oppressed and at their expense). The behavior is not assumed in response to the demands of formal or informal social control, but as a survival technique that allows one to hide inside the human herd. In these circumstances, the dominant modes of behavior are of an innovative, withdrawing, and rebellious character: innovative in the sense of trying to find new ways of adjusting to the harsh and cruel conditions of life; withdrawing in the sense of adopting apparently conformist behavior; and rebellious in the sense of trying to find a way of rejecting a domineering, oppressive framework. In consequence, the concept *instrumental* seems to be more suitable because, in a situation of oppression, the acting individual does not care about the generally accepted goals (as he or she does in the case of "innovative behavior"), but behaves in an elastic, plastic way (as in the case of "secondary adjustment"), searching for tactics that will provide the most suitable strategy of survival. Thus, under oppression the most common modes of behavior are the instrumental, withdrawal, and rebellious modes.

Thirdly, there are different areas where oppression manifests itself. Oppression takes place in the army, in the school, in the hospital, in prisons, and in many other social institutions. Although the forms of oppression that appear in various social settings have different characteristics, they can be divided according to the criteria of positive and negative and intended and unintended contexts. Intended negative oppression takes place in a concentration camp. The policy of a depersonalized, institutionalized unit could serve as an example of a personally unintended negative oppression. Here one may also formulate a general hypothesis concerning the relation of oppression caused by individuals and organizations in the modern world. The further the phenomenon and process of oppression are located from the interactions of small groups, in particular face-to-face encounters, then (a) the fewer the incidents of direct oppression and the lower the intensity of oppression triggered by individual feelings, and (b) the greater the oppression initiated by impersonal bodies (institutions, organizations, parties, etc.). The intended—or appearing as a by-product—oppression of the army, school, or hospital has its visible rationale: its discipline aims at predesigned effects.

It is not easy to find an example of an unintended positive oppression; Grygier's previously discussed determination to transform his existential position as one of the oppressed into an inquiry based on participatory observation could serve as an example. But from a theoretical point of view, the largely unexamined instances of unbound negative effects flowing from a supposedly positive oppression are theoretically especially interesting. Religious life sometimes demands a sharp sort of discipline. In the Roman Catholic Church, the constant preoccupation with sex clearly diverts the hierarchy of priorities, and the attention of its believers, from the demands of civil decency and honesty in political matters to moral sex sins. This diversion seems to be articulated and executed by the righteous indignation of those who are administratively deprived of sex and who envy those who can enjoy it.

One final point should be stressed. Independent of the volume and acuteness of an existing oppression, the human will, if it is persistent enough, can smash even the most overwhelming Moloch.

> But shouldn't I, at least, be experiencing a sense of joy? The joy of victory? No matter which way you looked at it, we had conducted a desperate war against this regime of utter scum. We were a handful of unarmed men facing a mighty State in possession of the most monstrous machinery of oppression in the entire world. And we had won. The State had been obliged to retreat. Even in jail we had proven too dangerous for it (Bukowski 1978: 342).

It seems clear that the study of oppressed behavior points to law as the essential social factor that molds various faces of oppressed behavior. If this analysis is correct, then it might be useful to study the peculiar type of law that is most pregnant with actual and potential features of oppression. By this criterion, *totalitarian law* appears as the most appropriate subject for further inquiry.

In the course of this inquiry, law should be understood not only as *official* law but also as *intuitive* law. Intuitive law is not based on written documents or the state's authority. Intuitive law is supported by mutually accepted understandings concerning respective claims and duties. Second, although totalitarian law concentrates on those features that are usually connected with oppression and are morally restrictive, this orientation could be misleading since strict self-discipline, while oppressive, is rather praiseworthy.

If rationality, as Weber indicates, is one of the most formalized features of social change, and if law is the most task-oriented instrument introducing rational types of social changes into social life, totalitarian law may be regarded as a pathological synthesis of these two primordial social factors. Since the study of social oppression generated by legal conformity is, by its very nature, a study of implemented social changes, any social oppression imposed by totalitarian law should be regarded as a study of social pressure amplified by powerful social factors like the educational system, the mass media, a centrally planned economy, the military complex, secret police, and a monopolistic and binding ideology.

The study of the social operation of a totalitarian legal system may thus be treated as an inquiry into the accumulated consequences of social oppression imposed on the macroscale. This study may also be taken as an investigation of laws constituting prerequisites of social changes that are not controlled by the pluralistically invoked and democratically regulated balance of conflicting social forces.

NOTE

1. Lanzmann.

4

Totalitarian Pathology of Law

To best understand totalitarianism, one should return to the work that heralded this, the worst man-made disaster in human history. In a short but poignant assertion, Popper (1945: 105) said:

> Ultimately, this claim [the totalitarian class rule of a naturally superior master race] is based upon the argument that justice is useful to the might, health, and stability of the state; an argument which is only similar to the modern totalitarian definition: right is whatever is useful to the might of my nation.

Crossman, a British member of Parliament who was educated and taught at Oxford, edited a book with a telling title, *The God That Failed*. At the close of his introduction, he states:

> But no one who has not wrestled with Communism as a philosophy and Communists as political opponents can really understand the values of Western Democracy. The Devil once lived in Heaven, and those who have not met him are unlikely to recognize an angel when they see it (Crossman 1950: 16).

It could be amended, however, that although in the West the road to appreciate Democracy was through a flirt with communism, in the East the road to Communist success led to Western opulence, and the fight with communism was the best way to comprehend it.

Crossman's book is dominated by an essay by Arthur Koestler. One of the most important points of this essay is the antitotalitarian statement, which stresses

> that man is a reality, mankind an abstraction; that men cannot be treated as units in operations of political arithmetic because they behave like symbols for zero and infinite, which dislocate all mathematical operations; that the end justifies the means only within very narrow limits; that ethics is not a function of social utility, and charity not a pretty-bourgeois sentiment but the gravitational force which keeps civilization in its orbit (Koestler 1950: 76).

Totalitarian oppression is especially discernible in the social functioning of the law. But this law would never have gained full swing, had the social climate and societal framework not reinforced its gravity.

Social oppression reaches its peak in the totalitarian regime. Such a regime is supposedly kept together by law. But it is a peculiar type of law: although it has all the formal characteristics of law, it is, in fact, only a facade used by the existing power.

The theoretical silence that currently surrounds even vivid descriptions of totalitarian and post-totalitarian institutions does not mean that their inherent totalitarian ramifications and potential dangers no longer exist. Therefore, it might be prudent to analyze the roots and consequences of these ramifications before they can reemerge.

Not long ago Friedrich and Brzezinski (1965) wrote a penetrating analysis of these phenomena. Indeed, in the sixties, totalitarianism was a very fashionable subject of scientific analysis. But after the violent Marxist claims that capitalist societies were totalitarian in an even more sophisticated and perverted way, interest in this issue subsided.

Recently, however, Brzezinski returned to this problem and tried to present an updated scheme of post-totalitarian development, distinguishing the following phases:

Phases in the retreat from Communism	Historical Status
Phase 1: Communism Totalitarianism. Communist party controls political system. Political system controls society and economy.	Albania North Korea Vietnam East Germany
Transition to Phase 2: Succession of struggles that divide ruling Communist party and increase societal pressure for socioeconomic concessions.	Rumania Cuba Czechoslovakia

Phase 2: Communism Authoritarianism. Communist party controls political system but emerging civil society contests it; political supremacy in the economy is on the defensive.

Soviet Union
China

Transition to Phase 3: Most likely by top-level coup in response to regime fears of rising social pressures; in some exceptional cases, directly to Phase 4; alternatively, if changes blocked, systemic fragmentation or repressive attempt to return to Phase 1.

Nicaragua
Hungary
Poland

Phase 3: Post-Communist Authoritarianism. Authoritarian regime based largely on national appeal; civil society becomes political society; political supremacy over economy in broad retreat.

Yugoslavia

Transition to Phase 4: Most likely turbulent in final stage of Phase 3, through peaceful evolution in some exceptional cases may be possible; alternatively, if change blocked, systemic fragmentation.

Phase 4: Post-Communist Pluralism. Political and socioeconomic systems become pluralistic (Brzezinski 1989: 255)

Brzezinski's scheme relies too heavily on political factors ("succession struggles" and "top-level coups") and does not sufficiently recognize social pressures that come from the bottom. Although, indeed, in Czechoslovakia political changes were triggered in 1989 by KGB agencies that tended to put this country in line with those transformations that took place in the "metropoly"; and while in the same year an inherent split in the Communist party of Hungary was precipitated as the result of a semi-top-level coup, the bulk of changes in Poland that heralded the antitotalitarian movement in Eastern Europe and the disintegration of the former Soviet Union were the result of internal, national, economic, cultural, or religious forces. Thus political and economic inefficiencies and crises in countries belonging to the Soviet Bloc seem to constitute the important causes of the disintegration of the Communist totalitarian empire. But social factors such as standardized conformity, hyperconformity, attitudinal "inertia," the cognitive-emotional cage that precludes a priori certain options, and the past imposition (if not imprinting) of patterns of behaviors that alone are deemed valid play an even more decisive role. Legal formal schemata provide these social factors with a matrix that helps to reinforce the vestiges of totalitarian or post-totalitarian systems.

On the basis of historical knowledge connected with studies of twentieth-century totalitarian systems, a cluster of concepts that characterize totalitarian law should be developed. In the future, this cluster could be used, among its other purposes, to help identify any new totalitarian developments, should they emerge.

Nevertheless despite the fact that legal systems in totalitarian and post-totalitarian regimes are now more open to scrutiny than hitherto, the specificity of these regimes is perhaps recognized mainly on a speculative and intuitive level. On the whole, the Kelsenian understanding of the law as a body of binding abstract rules imposed by political decision and arbitrarily formulated as a metanonlegal norm seems appropriate to describe the totalitarian hierarchy of the law. However, whereas the Kelsenian and Justinian conceptions of the law accept as an essential premise that the will of the sovereign (a body of undisclosed nature) gives origin to the whole system of building rules that are basically stable, the constituting feature of totalitarian law was its whimsicality and unpredictability. Laws may well be challenged in a sovereign democratic state, but only according to the principles that have been set by the requirements of the democratically generated metanorm (constitution). Challenges to the law in totalitarian regimes had no such guiding principles. There, changes arose from a hidden pattern that, on the surface, looks like a chaotic state of affairs.

Totalitarian regimes developed *sui generis* legal reasoning. This reasoning was so abstract, however, and so remote from social reality, that it was difficult, if not impossible, to state whether it was used to control the consistency of the legal system as a logically and normatively noncontradictory body of legal ideas or whether it was used as an instrument of an additional intellectual (pseudological) oppression. Works of internationally known scholars (for example: Opalek and Wroblewski, 1969) in the area of legal reasoning seem only to strengthen this otherwise purposely developed set of social traps (Mlicki 1991: 135–42).

The twentieth century has produced a plethora of totalitarian social and legal systems. Certain South American, Asian, and African systems may be characterized in this way, but the four most striking examples are Italian, German, Russian-Soviet, and Polish. What they have in common is as follows: (1) they emerged as modern products of European civilization and culture. "Totalitarian societies appear to be exaggerations, but nonetheless, logical exaggerations, of the technological state of modern society. . . . (T)he party, its leader(s), and the ideology link the totalitarian dictatorship to modern democracy" (Friedrich and Brzezinski 1965); (2) they were more or less connected with a phase of sophisticated development in bureaucratic structures; they are built according to the Weberian "rationality principle"; (3) they were the products of the First and Second World Wars and the sociopolitical crises associated with them; (4) they were characterized by the emergence of charismatic leaders; (5) they were also characterized by the rapid development and reception of the value-laden dogmas inherent in the approaches of aggressive political centers of populist parties. On the derivational level, these parties were busy producing ideological dogmas, and, on the residual level, elaborating new forms of social control and coercion exercised by the secret-police apparatus; (6) they were led by dictators who kept in their hands the wheels of secret-police power, and who also presented for followers and the general population a synthesis of obligatory ideologies that originated inside the party apparatus; and (7) politics shaped their economies.

> One of the great difficulties of conceptualizing totalitarianism arises from the great differences between the economic aspects of the Soviet system and those of the Nazi state. Both, nevertheless, have one thing in common. Both assert that the state has the right to direct all economic life, and in this they differ radically from laissez-faire liberalism. In the details of their activity, the two totalitarian regimes display striking economic differences; for example, the Soviet technique was expropriation, whereas the Nazis relied on extremely detailed regulation. In consequence, the political institution is the only employer in the Soviet Union, something which was not true in Germany (Timasheff in Friedrich 1954: 333).

The role of the law in all these countries has been enormously complicated. It has dealt for example, with the nationalization of land and industry in Soviet Russia, colonial expansion in Italy, revindication claims after World War I in Germany. The law also responded to several social transformations and these included (1) the rising awareness of suppressed national entities; (2) the urgent demands of the economically frustrated masses; (3) considerable support from ordinary police, secret police, and the state bureaucracy, as well as from the newly emerging social stratum of "red bourgeoisie" or *nomenklature*; (4) the unprecedented effectiveness of sociopolitical oppression combined with the rhetoric of social, economic, and political justice; (5) the unprecedented use of mass media as an agent of socialization processes; (6) the molding of the ideology and behavior of the legal profession in order to compel it to play the role of copartner against the forces of opposition; and (7) obliging social sciences to develop various forms of ideology in order to evolve, rationalize, and produce new forms of legitimation for state activities based on more or less visible criminal principles.

Using this general framework, I shall look more closely at the following aspects of totalitarian law:

- the "ground norm" of totalitarian law;
- the supremacy of the ground norm over the constitution;

- the servility of the totalitarian law;
- the "perverse" perfection of the totalitarian bureaucratization;
- oppression of and by the judiciary;
- "rule of law"—the derivational appearance of legalism;
- the popular appeal of harsh sanctions;
- legitimation;
- abuse of the citizen's point of view;
- law as an instrument of "dark" social engineering.

THE GROUND NORM

The basic norm of the totalitarian legal system is the will of the ruling elite disguised in the current ideological program. Totalitarian social systems produce power elites of various types. Some are visible elites; others are illusive so that the power is hidden behind their ranks and real powers. They may be of a capitalistic, militaristic, or even purely bureaucratic nature. Totalitarian ruling elites also tend to generate visible, charismatic figures who embody the elite's derivative ideology. Interrelations between charismatic totalitarian leaders and the intellectuals who serve them (by producing arguments in support of the basic ideological dogmas) are quite perplexing. Nonetheless, it should be stressed that both the leader and his/her hired experts are constantly engaged in the task of translating the current content of the basic totalitarian "ground norm" into a variety of sociopolitical impulses, such as enacting a new law, or interpreting or reinterpreting old. The undertaking is always for the "benefit of the whole."

Frequent statements that the basic norm of totalitarian social systems represents the will of the ruling elite are crude and primitive declarations. What does "will" mean? It means so many things that it might in the end mean nothing. When knights and aristocrats proclaimed the values of fatherland, monarchy, land, and religion, few of them realized, apparently, how shrewdly their own interests were masked by these declarations. The Spartans professed severe life ethics; capitalists profess the values of self-discipline and work, sometimes even welfare state politics. Hidden behind each of these notions, however, was a clear emphasis on success. Throughout the history of humankind, knights, aristocrats, and capitalists have been convinced that the values they proclaimed were beneficial for their respective societies. In the case of totalitarian elites, the situation is entirely different.

Relatively few members of these elites actually believe in the values they so eagerly and skillfully promulgate. The overwhelming majority of them are fully aware that they impose on others a false ideology in their own interest. This is the metalaw of totalitarian social systems.

Empirical data concerning these problems are not available. If they existed, they might show that only a tiny number of the oppressed believe in this ideology. The pressures of an orchestrated mass media and of the educational system, intimidation, punishment, and the sheer repetition of dogmas transform purely normative into semireal ideology, and give rise to false consciousness. The net effect of all these socializing measures is to create a near-omnipotent machinery of persuasion that translates the totalitarian ground norm into various types of legal enactments, decrees, ordinances, regulations, and social conformity that they generate.

TOTALITARIAN GROUND NORM VERSUS A CONSTITUTION

In a fascist or a communist society, the constitution is imposed on the population as a facade document of national importance. It does not list those rights that are practiced by citizens, but it enumerates as norms that ought to be valid those norms that are desired. These "strong" elements of totalitarian law contain dormant seeds of future weakness.

The ruling elite uses the mere existence of the constitution as proof that its citizenry enjoys assumed privileges. This amounts to a spectacular jump from normative reality into factual reality, from "ought" to "is." In some instances, the ruling elite might concede that there are some discrepancies between normative and real rights, but the acknowledgement is used only to distract attention from the chasm that separates these phenomena; to divert attention from the shadow constitution that proclaims that only those norms of the facade-constitution that have the current *placet* of the party apparatus can be regarded as valid. Sometimes a "compromise" between normative reality and factual reality is established. In the Soviet Union, for instance, the constitution had a provision according to which the Communist party was regarded as hegemonic over the constitution and society. Strangely enough, in 1976, "civil society" in Poland defended the previous Stalinist constitution against attempts to introduce a provision of this type. Paradoxically, when the Polish "Stalinist" constitution was enacted in 1952, the party was not prepared to be so openly arrogant as to claim that it was above the constitution, whereas Polish civil society was too much terrorized to oppose the constitution.

In 1976 the situation was different. The Polish Communist party, having achieved nothing of substance in the area of socioeconomic life, wanted to create an illusion that it had some real accomplishments to its credit. Therefore, the party used the technique: normative is regarded as "real." Additionally, the party misjudged the actual strength of Polish civil society and had made an inadequate diagnosis of its own weaknesses. But the fundamental premise underlying this course of action was proven faulty in a number of ways. It was assumed, for example, that the Polish population had actually internalized the Marxist dogmas that had been imposed on it. This false assumption was maintained and nourished by the arrogance of the ruling elite's false consciousness. Alienated from the society through the accelerated accumulation of privileges and transformed into the "red bourgeoisie," this Communist power center was seen by the general population as a group of oppressors united by direct access to the instruments of coercion. But the power elite, seduced by its own philosophy, persisted in claiming a fundamental commonality between its own interests and society's best interests. Needless to say, this conviction operated only on the derivational level.

Thus, the totalitarian constitution, with or without a clause asserting the dominant role of the party, was intended to create an impression that the basic norms on which it was built were identical with the benefit of the society as a whole.

Totalitarian law is ingenious indeed in finding ways to circumvent the spirit of the law. Peterson gives the following illustration of this point.

Two days after Franco's election on September 29, 1936, by the wartime Junta de Defensa National as the chief of the Government of the Spanish State, he made use of the fact that he had been endowed with "all the powers of the State" (Payne 1987: 116) and promulgated the first law over his signature establishing the Government of the Technical Council (41). In the Law of Central Administration enacted on January 30, 1938, Franco reconstructed the Government and "reserved for himself the promulgation of *laws* (basic general legislation) and *decrees* (implementing laws or [laws dealing with] less general subjects)... [a move which] amounted to the absorption or assimilation of the legislative power by the executive (Peterson 1991: 22).

SERVILITY OF THE LAW

Totalitarian social systems do not treat law in a way that is autotelic, or valid for itself. This means that the law does not have a normative value on its own: since it is not independent, there is no exclusive area that belongs to it alone. Totalitarian law is constantly dependent. In short, it is heterotelic, or valid for reasons existing outside. In other words, official totalitarian law can be regarded as normatively valid only if a higher, political norm provides it with the final and decisive placet and furnishes it with power of a political nature. Schmidt (1991: 4) gives a good example:

Hans F. Scholl, Sophia M. Scholl, and Christoph Probst, students of the University of Munich, most known dissidents in the Third Reich, produced and distributed flyers. They have been accused to ask in their fliers for sabotage of the armament and the overthrowing of the national-socialistic way of life of the people, to propagate defeatist ideas, and to insult the Führer in a very malicious way and thereby to support the enemy of the Reich and to decompose the defensive force. The *VOLKSGERICHTSHOF*, Senate, considers their actions suited to destroy the defensive force, and decides on February 22, 1943: Sophia Scholl, Hans Scholl, and Christoph Probst are dishonourable for ever and will be punished to death. They have been decapitated in the afternoon of the same day. The law on which these sentences have been based, was official, positive, written law, enacted to support the system under consideration.

As a rule, without this type of political approval, law cannot be regarded as valid. If a Communist party member commits a crime, he or she cannot be brought to court, even if his/her guilt is evident, without the permission of the relevant party organs. Indeed, in order to receive high office in the state bureaucracy, there has to be a political decision to ensure that the appointment is appropriate. If this position is reserved for the so-called *nomenklatura*, then clearance has to come directly from the party's ideological headquarters.[1] In a totalitarian social system, practically all legal norms and legal institutions have their own "shadow" counterparts. A given norm is valid only as long as it is not in disagreement with its shadow character. A given institution may function only if, after monitoring by its shadow agency, it gets a green light. At first glance, one might think that the totalitarian legal system does not differ from any other, including democratic legal systems. But this is not the case, since the shadow counterpart of any legal norm, although decisive for its validity, is quite difficult to find.

The shadowy counterlegal system plays an omnipresent and decisive role. It constantly reminds the population that the law is an instrument used by the current political power. The law can be changed (more euphemistically "adapted," "adjusted," or "modernized") according to the actual desires of the power elite. According to totalitarian doctrine, the ruling elite represents the collective wisdom of those who are the subjects of the law. If it sometimes appears that the law or changes in the law are not beneficial for the populace, this is attributed to "faulty perception" on the part of biased critics or to their incomprehension or partial comprehension based on limited access to data. Their skepticism is seen as a kind of false comprehension; had they been able to comprehend the data in a more holistic way, they would surely agree with those who do see the matter from the more global, balanced, and many-sided perspective of the party. The ruling elite, with its enlarged perspective, is in a position to shape the desires of its populace in a way that is beneficial not only for the present desires of living subjects but also for future generations. If the subjects are skeptical about that, they have to be "persuaded," "educated," or punished. Punishments are seen as propitious for skeptics, for they are being socialized for their own good.

Totalitarian law tends, when possible, not to be overtly servile. This servility thus tends not to be mechanical; rather, it is designed to capture the imagination and appeal to the collective wisdom and spirit of those it exploits to make them believe that what is done is done for their benefit. Therefore, the vested interests of power-keepers compel them, for their own sake, to perform the task of spreading false consciousness efficiently.

TOTALITARIAN BUREAUCRATIZATION

A special study should be undertaken to show that each bureaucracy shares several characteristics with a totalitarian legal system. Even a bureaucracy in a democratic society is totalitarian to a certain degree, because each bureaucracy contains the germ of a holistic, rationally restricting, impersonal approach. This is due not only to the hierarchical nature of bureaucracies but to the organizational principles that they entail. When an individual is surrounded by anonymous agencies, when he is treated everywhere in an impersonal way, and when he is reified, then even a democratic sociopolitical framework may not help him much. He or she feels himself/herself to be in a Kafkaesque void, becoming helplessly exposed to administrative omnipotence.

Bureaucracy, however, may also hold some advantages for an individual, such as providing an assurance of impartiality and rationality. To be impartial and just, bureaucracy has to be impersonal, but this quality in itself may be a destructive force. A clerk who is not interested (and who is not allowed to be interested) in the personal features of his/ her client, and whose attention is focused instead on the rational logic of the matter, will act in a more detached way than he or she would if an official were personally involved. The client, however, who has had no experience of the legal system or its procedure, abhors the social system that tends to treat him or her as an element without human feelings, bonds, and ties. This individual experiences overwhelming conformist pressure of norms, institutions, organizations, and rituals that bring him or her to the edge of personal disintegration.

If rationally developed bureaucracies in democratic societies can exert such a destructive influence on the individual, the situation of a citizen in a totalitarian sociolegal setting is much more devastating. Totalitarian law is very skillful in depersonalizing human beings.

Here, for example, the SPD member of the Reichstag, Kunt, is taken away on the craft, surrounded by SA troopers, to be "interrogated." *Symbolic terror* is a subtle affair. To have to sit on a kind of manure cart, in full view of the public, while dressed in one's best clothes is humiliating in the extreme. Here we have a person viewed with disdain as "one of those high-ups" who, so this situation suggests, will no longer have the privilege of his chauffeur-driven car, for he is sitting on the knacker's cart which will take him to the place of execution, even though there is, "first of all," supposed to be an interrogation (Gephart 1990: 7).

Totalitarian sociolegal systems not only treat an individual as a constantly crushed entity, an entity constantly oppressed by the alienating forces of these systems and their ramifications; the law itself develops additional measures to oppress an individual. First, the bureaucracy in totalitarian sociolegal systems is corrupt, one-sided, and evidently working for the benefit of the ruling elite. Hence it does not give an individual a feeling of protection; on the contrary, it threatens him. Therefore, the individual has to strive for personal survival and fight against the bureaucratic forces working for the smooth operation of hidden powers. Second, bureaucratic systems in sociolegal totalitarian settings do not provide, as they occasionally do in democratic surroundings, access to professional, sometimes free, legal aid. If such aid does exist, then it is arranged in a way that puts pressure on lawyers to support the system, and only lawyers who are willing to cooperate are hired. Third and most important, totalitarian systems develop a complicated web of informal, social-control devices that surround an individual and compel him or her to act according to the expectations of Medusa.

In China, for example, the state monitors the sex lives of females in order to control the excessive increase of the population. State bureaucracy sets certain limits regarding birth rate, with different limits for various sections of the population, and develops several educational and technical measures to achieve these goals. Since some measures are not efficient enough, bureaucracy additionally develops certain informal mechanisms such as neighborhood committees, to achieve these goals.

The Residents' Committee of each district was an extension of the police department, working under its supervision. Officers of the Residents' Committee dealt directly with the people and reported to the police. The organization was responsible for the weekly political indoctrination of the residents, running the day-care centres, distributing ration coupons, allocating birth quotas, and arbitrating disputes between neighbors. In some instances, officers of the Residents' Committee even helped the police solve crimes and capture criminals, as they had such an intimate knowledge of the life of the people in their charge. Most of the officers of the Residents' Committee were retired workers on government pensions, receiving no pay for their present work. Only in special cases, when the retirement pension was low, were the officers given an additional allowance. These ladies (and a few men) enjoyed great power over the people. Their reports on each individual were treated as confidential and were written into the dossiers kept by the police. In fact, the Residents' Committee system enabled the police to remain in the background while maintaining close and constant surveillance of the entire population (Cheng 1986: 378).

In the Soviet Union, school-pupil organizations are set up to control the sociopolitical behavior of parents; in Poland after World War II, each workplace had its own party "cell," which closely observed the behavior of those working there. In Nazi Germany, neighborhood committees monitored the behavior of all who happened to fall within the committee's ambit. In general, in totalitarian societies, informants are treated as people who have the civil courage to overstep the bounds of traditional morality and provide the state authorities with much-needed information to evaluate, change, correct, or eliminate certain types of behavior, officially regarded as deviant.

In effect, in the sociopolitical conditions of totalitarian societies an individual is not only exposed to the crushing pressures of the impersonal Cronus of institutional omnipotence, but is additionally checked from below by the organized web of personal, informal, flexible, penetrating interhuman relations existing inside the family and neighborly communities. Thus, the formal machinery sets into motion a more efficient informal one.

The interplay between the impersonal structure of totalitarian bureaucracies and their informal agencies that control human behavior in an antibureaucratic way gives rise to the interesting but only partially recognized phenomenon of *totalitarian fiefdoms*. A totalitarian economy is, as a rule, inefficient. The populations of totalitarian societies live under the constant pressure of everyday needs, and practically everybody lives under the dominance of several tall, crosscutting pyramids of discretion belonging to the powerful. In this situation, a peculiar tendency emerges: the tendency to create for oneself, inside one's own field of discretion, a domain that enables one to oppress others.

In any case, I was fortunate; the woman official did not refuse to give me the application form. If she had refused, there was absolutely nothing I could have done except to give up the whole idea of applying. Although her position in the bureaucratic structure could not have been very senior, the power she was allowed to exercise seemed frighteningly enormous (Cheng 1986: 503).

This kind of oppression allows a person to take subtle satisfaction in the harm that has been done to him/her because it "justifies" his/her doing it to others. In short, in order to reestablish psychological equilibrium, a totalitarian citizen projects his/her suffering onto others and tries to transfer the aggression that constantly plagues him/her to his/her fellow citizens. He or she perversely enjoys the power that, in this way, he/she wields. Since practically everybody in a totalitarian society operates as a government official, everybody has his/her own field, or fiefdom, in which he/she can exercise a sort of monopolistic power. On the lowest level, he/she may or may not sell a magazine of a limited circulation to a potential buyer; it is up to him/her to decide whether the buyer looks submissive enough to earn him/her this favor (the majority of vendors act as agents of the government's selling firms).

The phenomenon of totalitarian fiefdoms is constructed by the use of bureaucratic authority to expose others to the dance of rewards and punishments that may, at least partially, compensate for totalitarian oppression.

OPPRESSION OF, AND BY, THE JUDICIARY

Totalitarian social systems recognize the divisions between legislative, executive, and judicial branches of government only pro forma. The judiciary is, of course, the most visible victim of this political aggression. According to the traditional doctrine in democratic societies, the judiciary should check the balance of two other powers, observing whether or not the legislative and executive divisions exceed their given authority. In totalitarian social systems, the judiciary possesses no such power, but is used, on the contrary, as an additional measure to control the citizenry. How is this done?

When I visited China in 1963, I expressed a wish to meet a judge. This proved difficult. I was informed that there were only a few judges in the whole country. Apparently, judges were not in great demand, since the neighborhood committees had the capacity and power to solve an overwhelming majority of legal problems that arose in local communities. To explain this situation better, I was told the following story. In one district, a young person, due to his intellectual skills and mature political attitudes was appointed as a judge. He was a good judge, and regardless of his age, was able to solve even the most complicated cases. Though he had no formal legal education, he was capable of supporting his judgements by his own intuitive understanding of the law. On a few occasions, when he perceived that a case was beyond the scope of his personal wisdom, he would go to the party secretary for advice. Although in 1991 this story is no longer fully characteristic of China, it gives a clear illustration of the relation between the judiciary and the party in a totalitarian country.

The logistical arrangements that assure the dominance of the party are relatively simple and similar in various totalitarian countries. Judges are appointed for a specific period of time (in Poland for five years, as a rule). Every year, and especially towards the end of their appointments, they are carefully assessed not only on the number of cases they have completed, their legal competence, and the speed with which they work but also, and above all, on the political content of their sentences. The Ministry of Justice (or other institution at this level) sends policy instructions to judges. They specify social problems that are especially acute at any given moment, provide a diagnosis (tentative and superficial) of these problems, and recommend the adoption of a certain policy (as a rule, stiffer sentences). Additionally, judges are constantly monitored by their supervisors (judges of a higher rank) as to whether or not they apply these recommendations. Supervisors also have access to the political profiles of judges, and they instruct administrators to take account of these profiles when they are allocating politically sensitive cases. Thus, if a politically significant case appears in court, it would go to the judge who could give an assurance that he (or she—women constitute, at least in Poland, an increasing proportion of judges) would give a sentence that complied with the current party line. Judges are poorly paid, moreover, which preselects to the profession only those who exhibit lower professional capabilities (as compared, for example, with advocates). They are also more malleable.[2]

On the whole, then, the judiciary in a totalitarian social system serves as an additional filter that selects legal norms as appropriate for officially approved goals. This filter omits certain norms (and could even deny the defendant the right to have a defense lawyer), neutralizes certain norms (the judge may reinterpret motions made by the defendant), and emphasizes certain rules (the judge may extend his/her inquisitorial power beyond the limits that are usually prescribed for the parties). Generally speaking, the totalitarian legal system uses the judiciary to invoke, promote, and channel conformist behavior, which is beneficial for the state and oppressive for the citizenry.

THE APPEARANCE OF LEGALITY

Law in totalitarian societies is not applied according to its meaning or according to its letter. The preconceived spirit of the law is more important than the law itself. Interpretation of content and understandings of context are constantly changed to reflect politically changeable situations. Consequently, the real meaning of the law constantly fluctuates, trembles, jumps, and engages in various topsy-turvy acrobatics. As a result, the general public in Communist countries knows quite well that it would be a great mistake to expect the law to have a constant, fixed meaning (Łoś 1988). The ruling elite appears to be aware of the negative image of the law in the public eye and counteracts this image by insisting that, in totalitarian countries, everything is done according to the letter of the law. Thus, the ruling elite creates an artificial language and a spurious way of thinking, according to which the law should be regarded as the guiding rule of the state. Additionally, it plays a facade function. "The facade of the Soviet government, despite its written constitution, is even less impressive, erected even more exclusively for foreign observation than the state administration which the Nazis inherited and retained from the Weimar Republic" (Arendt, quoted by Mason 1967: 55). Everyone is familiar with this fiction.[3] Nonetheless, everyone is under pressure to conform. As a consequence, two parallel realities exist: the reality of instability, unpredictability, and the systematic misuse of the law; and the reality of "socialist governance" of the law, or "communist legality," or the "rule of law."

With the passage of time, people begin to know how to use the language of the first and second categories of reality. They tend to use the first language in small, well-trusted private circles while reserving the second language for official settings alone. But with the constant "improvement" of measures of social control, a confusing lack of knowledge about the law, increasing uncertainty about who is who, and the use of random "preventive" punishments, official control penetrates even the close face-to-face interrelations of private circles. Then it becomes unsafe to apply the first language. The official language gains the upper hand. The general population gradually becomes accustomed to it, starts to use it as a safety measure, and therefore approves this official language. Eventually, the official language infiltrates people's private lives to such an extent that, in order to utter even the most trivial and banal truth about the real functioning of the law, one has to show considerable civil courage.

> All laws and regulations have been declared tools of the "capitalist-roaders" against the people. No one knows what's legal and what's illegal any more. I suppose when one gets caught, it's illegal. When one gets away with it, it's legal. People using the back door seem to get away with it, so everybody does it (Cheng 1986: 365).

In consequence, the artificial language based on fiction becomes the natural one, and the true language based on a careful reading of social reality becomes the controversial one. It is only when there is sudden social change or a social catastrophe that the public begin to discuss more independently and to question whether or not the concept of legality is indeed based on the law or only on some whimsical invention of the ruling elite.

LEGITIMATION

Max Weber highlighted the problem of legitimation in his attempt to describe and classify legitimacy in its various forms. According to him, *charismatic* legitimacy is based on the personal features of the leader. These features are directly connected with his/her unusual qualifications and spectacular performances. Thus, he/she compels his/her followers to believe in the importance of his/her leading role in performing a higher mission. *Traditional* domination has its roots in the master's authority over his household and may manifest itself in patrimonial or feudal forms. Patrimonial dominance is more personal, being determined by direct contact with the master. Feudal dominance additionally contains some impersonal and formal elements generated by the elaborate rank system. *Legal-rational* legitimacy is based on the crucial feature of the "impersonality of legal norm." The best summary of Weber's ideas about different types of legitimation is in Bendix (1977).

Weber's classification, revealing as it is, has some weaknesses, however. It provides no common principle of division and does not adequately fit social reality. It does not, for example, include totalitarian forms of legitimation.

Totalitarian legal systems are based on what might be called *dead-end* legitimacy. Sometimes the citizenry may tolerate the government it does not respect, thus indirectly legitimizing its authority. This paradoxical situation may arise when the populace feels that the existing power structure is possibly less harmful than the alternatives. For example, if previous attempts to overthrow the existing authority (which may have been installed by outside forces) failed, ending in disaster and reinforcing the view that fighting the existing regime makes a bad situation worse; when the population has no established tradition of fighting for its freedom; when it is obvious that the superior power that imposed the hated rules and rulers is more than a match for the forces of the subjugated society; when coalition with the other conquered societies does not seem feasible; when the international situation militates against a possible collapse of the superior power; when the fear of repression in response to increased opposition seems too unbearable: all these factors may lead to a situation of peculiar constraint. This type of *a rebours* legitimacy generates pessimism, a sense of impotence, passivity, and, in effect, may even lead to a compliance with a particular regime.

Prolonged experience of this type of oppressive rule may give rise to the emergence of an entirely new type of legitimacy, especially when transmission of cultural heritage to new generations is successfully blocked by harsh social control.

Natural legitimacy, or *legitimacy supported by false consciousness*, would surface when citizens start to regard the existing government as something natural, a given, like the weather. Knowing no other options, being unfamiliar with any other forms of government, cultural patterns, life-styles, or basic values, the citizenry may come to take the status quo as much for granted as the change from day to night. In fact, this is the dream of the ideal model of the totalitarian state (Podgórecki 1985).

In the case of legitimacy supported by false consciousness, excessive forms of social control are unnecessary. False consciousness might be so cunningly implanted in the citizens' psyches that they begin to regard the "gift" of the totalitarian regime as an inherent element in their souls. Social control of this type costs the regime very little. Once injected into the individual, propaganda starts to operate as an independent element of a metaego (or superego), as a compass guiding behavior and shaping its evaluations. Therefore Ellul is right when he insists that totalitarian propaganda must be distinguished from any discussion of the phenomenon of propaganda as it appears in democratic societies. Its monopolistic exclusiveness, continuous repetitiveness, hidden agenda, and unchallenged manipulativeness are decisive (Ellul 1967).

Open societies are becoming increasingly aware of the extent to which they, too, are shaped by "propaganda," albeit of a different sort and with different aims. The levelling of individuality under the bulldozer of consumerism is one of the phenomena that is rather well recognized. Totalitarian propaganda is not so much concerned with the spending of one's own resources, but it is preoccupied with the monopolistic shaping of individual selves, and by making them apparently concerned with the ideas regarding the whole of mankind, shape them, in fact, to be instrumental for the ruling elite. This type of social control appears almost exclusively in closed societies, especially when they tightly close off both physical and informational borders. But when the gates of these social systems are even slightly opened, inculcated false consciousness and respectful and cheap social control disappear quickly.

"Dark" social engineering uses social sciences to employ seemingly beneficial means to achieve goals that are rejected by the population at large. Since this type of social engineering does not disclose its real goals, it tries to transform the alienated legal system (beneficial for the elite, and harmful for the population) into a legal system supported by internalized values. This strategy, if successful, may have some advantages for its users: (1) it may help to transform totalitarian values into social reality; (2) it may help to weaken the consciousness of the existing socioeconomic conflict between the rulers and their subjects; and (3) it may minimize (as indicated above) use of the mighty and expensive apparatus of social control.

It is important to note that, when defending themselves against totalitarian impositions, societies sometimes produce certain social phenomena that, in the short run, help them to survive the current oppression. In the long run, however, these social phenomena paradoxically engender support for oppressive regimes. *Dirty togetherness*, discussed in Chapter 2 in connection with the workings of the Instrumental self, is one such phenomenon (see also Podgórecki and Łoś 1979: 202–3).

THE APPEAL OF HARSH SANCTIONS

Totalitarian social systems, as a rule, use harsh legal sanctions. They apply these sanctions mainly as a deterrent device that is designed to prevent people from doing what is regarded by the ruling elite as negative. Negative does not mean, in this context, socially harmful. One reason why such rigid sanctions work in these systems is that they appeal to public opinion, which in matters of punishment is almost everywhere harsh (even in democratic England). The second reason is more complicated. It concerns the well-established regularity in sociology of law that notices an inclination among those who come from the lower social strata to be more severe in their judgements and in their readiness to use more oppressive sanctions. In totalitarian societies, the ruling elites are often composed of those who belong, from a social point of view, at the bottom of the social ladder. This can create a unique type of social consensus between the ruling elite and the social strata from which they come. Thus, a specific "double reinforcement" takes place here that, in turn, has implications with respect to the use of denunciation as a form of condemnation.

Different types of denunciation are in use. One type is directed against human actions that are representative of social problems that are regarded as negative. This type of denunciation is perceived as the humiliation of an individual, but is meant to signal rejection of the individual's behavior. Thus, if a judge denounces an individual in his/her sentence, he or she discloses to the public that the motives, values, life-style, and behavior of the given individual are socially harmful, and devastating to his/her actual or potential victims. The judge does not use the verdict as a destructive weapon against the person; rather the judge is performing a public duty in revealing the dormant evils of the behavior in question (Walker 1969: 19–21).

This type of denunciation is used in open societies mainly as a teaching performance. But the insistence on harsh sanctions as an accompaniment in totalitarian societies adds new meaning to public denunciation. In these societies, denunciation is directed not only against the offender but also against the sociopolitical values that this person may embody. Public "degradation ceremonies" (Garfinkel 1965: 420–24) in order to be successful and to invoke group solidarity have to fulfill the following eight conditions: (1) the perpetrator and the event must be removed from the realm of the ordinary world; (2) the event must be generalized to describe a type of event, not the factual event itself; (3) the denouncer must be seen as an official figure; (4) denouncement must be done with respect to the values of the community (or group); (5) the denouncer must speak in the name of these values (not in relation to wrongs done to him or her); (6) the denouncer must be perceived as a supporter of community (or group) values; (7) the denouncer must be seen as socially distanced from the denounced; and (8) the denounced must be estranged from the community. Although degradation ceremonies that took place in China during the Cultural Revolution were different from "classical" degradation ceremonies in the respect that the denounced have not been entirely estranged from the community, the ceremonies were socially engineered not only to undercut the authority of party officials belonging to the wrong faction, but also to destroy their personal integrity. Denunciation of certain roles was designed to discourage people from adopting such roles in the future.

Denunciation is also used in totalitarian countries as a means of getting personal revenge: a citizen, usually anonymously, might inform the authorities about the unlawful behavior of his/her hated neighbor, relative, competitor, or other enemy. Generally speaking, denunciation is a tool of dark social engineering, which replaces disintegrated social ties and creates a void with formalized regulations.

Lukes (1977: 262) noticed the link between the totalitarian type of government and the use of harsh penalties:

> Where absolute governments existed, political offenses were seen as sacrilegious and were violently repressed, and all offenses tended to become political and to be seen as attacks on the sovereign. Thus "the gravity of most crimes is raised by several degrees; as a result the average intensity of punishments is greatly strengthened." This, one may say, was Durkheim's theory of charisma, and the nearest he came to developing a theory of totalitarianism.

ABUSE OF THE CITIZEN'S POINT OF VIEW

From the citizen's point of view, totalitarian law is a contradiction in terms. To begin with, totalitarian law does not offer stability. What is decided one day may be changed tomorrow. For example, in the 1960s some people of Polish origin decided to return to Poland for their retirement. They made this decision with the intention of capitalizing on the high exchange rate of "hard currencies." A retirement pension that would keep them near subsistence level in the West would allow them, in Poland, to enjoy a high standard of living. They lost out, however, because the regulations were quickly changed, and the official rate of exchange was converted to a low level.

In addition, totalitarian law frequently violates the cardinal metarule of the law: *lex retro non agit* (law does not impose its validity on the past). In Poland, after World War II, a new criminal law was enacted. According to this law, those who participated in anticommunist activities before the war were treated as criminals. Several people were tried, sentenced, and executed. Some of the survivors (and nonsurvivors) of this purge were later rehabilitated, thanks to fluctuations in the political situation. A similar situation prevailed under the fascist regime:

> The principle of non-retroactivity of law is no longer recognised. In many cases, the law-giver has issued retroactive laws, such as the lex Van der Lubbe of 29th March, 1934, which extended the death penalty to certain crimes committed between 31st January and 28th February, 1933; the law of 14th July, 1933, empowering the Minister to repeal naturalisation and to deprive Germans of their citizenship; the law of 3rd July, 1934, retroactively making legal certain decrees and administrative acts; and finally, the law of 3rd July, 1934, legalising all measures undertaken for the crushing of the Rochm revolt, a law which for the first time in history did not declare a past action illegal, but made legal an already-committed crime (Neumann 1986: 293–94).

Finally, several areas of social life that were previously regulated by customs, habits, and mutual informal agreements are transformed, under the regime of totalitarian law, into criminal behavior. This is attributable not only to ideologically bound changes in the conceptual understanding of criminal law but also, and largely, to the desire to extend the influence of the aggressive official law over the traditional private spheres of personal life.

Unexpected and frequent change in the law arouses in the population a strong feeling of distrust; it generates a lack of confidence not only in the law itself but in all its allied agencies. Although in normal circumstances such anxiety is highly dysfunctional (conflict-prone, confusing, not conducive to long-term planning, etc.), the totalitarian decisions makers, being aware of the hidden potential of this apprehension, tend to use it to their own advantage (see, for example, Tejchma 1991). They welcome the growing level of social insecurity, regarding it as an additional instrument of more effective manipulation. By their calculations, fear should penetrate the society's infrastructure and infiltrate the very basis of the "civil society." Harsh penalties, quietly functioning cadres of invisible informers, efficient Medusa-like activities of the bureaucratic apparatus, swift and massive retaliation by social-control forces against the sociopolitical opposition, and, above all, the whimsical and unexpected interventions of the law itself are designed to enmesh the already disintegrated psyche of the individual and paralyze his/her antigovernmental intentions.

These factors contribute to the creation of an atmosphere of general social nihilism, which further develops the widespread "culture" of instrumentality. The individual acquires a feeling that he/she can rely only on his/her own capabilities and is therefore compelled to use all available resources for his/her own advantage.

It is characteristic of the totalitarian ruling elite that it incorporates, at one and the same time, two ambiguous points of view. Openly it maintains that it is the true avant-garde of an adoring population, but it understands tacitly that the population hates it. Straddling these two points of view, the totalitarian ruling elite regards intimidation as highly effective, especially when it is coupled with constantly intoned rhetoric concerning its "undisputed" dominance.

From the citizen's point of view, the imposition of unjust legal enactments and the anxiety engendered by the whimsical functioning of the legal system may lead to a deepening sense of anomie, or to political revolt.

LAW AS AN INSTRUMENT OF "DARK" SOCIAL ENGINEERING

There are several distinct types of social engineering: (1) sociotechnics proper—the theory of efficient social action or, more correctly, an applied social science based on the paradigm of efficient social action; (2) self-made social engineering, which presupposes the existence of verified knowledge concerning the effectiveness of social activities based on an accumulated and generalized professional experience; (3) "quackish" social engineering, which differs from the self-made model in that it pretends to be competent by formulating practical recommendations, when in fact it is unfamiliar with the real, tested, and relevant theoretical framework; and (4) "dark" social engineering, which is the conscious use of sociotechnics proper or self-made social engineering to produce sociopolitical harm (Podgórecki 1989).

Regimes of a totalitarian character have developed quite advanced strategies of dark social engineering along with many semirational rationalizations and derivations. For example, in Poland after World War II, the Academy of Sciences was established as a model for the development of sciences and the progress of scientific "work." The academy is peculiar in a number of ways. It does not provide a regular meeting place for the exchange of ideas among the most prominent scholars. Rather, it constitutes a huge bureaucratic machinery that allocates resources according to political criteria. Moreover, despite the massive support that it receives, the academy produces little scientific work—the overwhelming majority of Ph.D. theses or "habilitations" (theses of a higher rank than Ph.D.) are generated at universities. The academy primarily supports the social sciences and humanities, since these disciplines are easier to manipulate than the natural sciences or mathematics. Finally, the academy is run by administrative fiat, which not only contradicts the spirit of the scientific community but also provides politicians with immediate access to the processes and procedures of elaborating the results of scientific "work." Politicians can thus tailor these results according to their current political wishes since achievements in social sciences and humanities cannot be tested in a strict, empirical way. The tailoring can be done by administrative recommendation, by persuasion of various types, or even by sheer force. One can see the influence of dark social engineering, for instance, when the high standards of the Academy of Learning established after World War I (a counterpart of the British Royal Academy) are attributed to the current model. The communist Academy of Sciences pretends to generate, in social sciences and humanities, "products" of a high standard, when, in fact, it generates only mediocre results. This result is mainly due to rewards that enhance politically conformist attitudes, a general lack of measures for testing the ideas that emerge, and the premeditated abuse of the respect that attaches to the former academy and comparable institutions around the world.

This elaborate example was intended to show how legal, institutional arrangements may influence certain areas of social life. Thus, the law may decide through its administrative measures what is "good" and what is "bad"; what is "healthy" and what is "pathological"; and law may determine the logistics of dealing with phenomena that have been defined as "positive" and those that are regarded as "deviant." Dark social engineering sometimes appears as a criminal arrangement. Creation of *Judenrats* was an unusually drastic example of this type of engineering. Then "technicians" (as they have been described by Steiner and Lanzmann) used organizational (not technical) tools to achieve their goals.

The second section, titled *Judisshe Alterstenrate* (Councils of Jewish Elders), prescribed that a Jewish council be established in each community to carry out the instructions of the *Einsatzgruppen* [it was prepared by several persons, including Rudolf Diels, the first Gestapo chief, and Dr. Johannes von Leers, a professor of history, and "expert" on the Jews]. It was to consist of available "influential personalities and rabbis." The idea of a Jewish council headed by an "Eldest" (*Alteste*) probably derived from the practice in medieval Germany, when the internal affairs of the Jewish community were regulated by so-called *Judenbischof*, "bishop of the Jews," in fact, chief rabbi. He was assisted by an advisory council of twelve *dayanim*, composing a *Judenrat*, all usually chosen or elected by the tax-paying members of the community and approved by the Emperor (Dawidowicz 1975: 116–17).

In some instances, this dark social engineering was developed to macroproportions. Exploiting the ghetto in Lodz, where the community of 200,000 Jews was working between September 1942 and September 1944 (when the ghetto was liquidated and almost all of its inhabitants killed), the Germans accumulated remarkable profit.

In addition to the tons of munitions, telecommunication equipment, uniforms, boots, lingerie, temporary housing, carpets and all manner of other goods the Germans extracted from the Jewish laborers, Berlin had a net profit of 46,211,485 Reichsmarks from the ghetto, following its final liquidation. The Jews had certainly demonstrated to the Germans that they were not "parasites." The ghetto had worked instead as a giant war industry, arming its enemy (Adelson and Lapides 1989: xix).

In conclusion, when the law is working in tandem with dark social engineering, it acquires a criminal character, losing in this way its basic and most essential feature—its principled character of impartiality.

THEORETICAL IMPLICATIONS

In accordance with the classical Roman conception, the law is binding when the parties concerned agree to specify their respective duties and rights. The concept of intuitive law assumes that the balance between duties and claims is regarded by the involved parties as mutually advantageous. Of course, there are exceptions, but mainly in the realm of official law. If someone makes a contract with his/her partner in bad faith, or misleads his/her partner about the essential element of the contract, then the agreement can be regarded as void. In such situations, a metanorm cancels the validity of norms of a lower order. While these metainterventions are exceptional, they are nevertheless incorporated into the body of the binding law as its corrective, well-established components. Metanorms of this type are norms belonging to the system of official law and cannot be invoked without clear reference to the clause that establishes their existence. In nontotalitarian legal systems, the official law is based on rights and duties that link together two corresponding parties; legal reciprocity pertains not only to the partners who are connected by mutually agreed contract. People engaged in a legal relationship are not necessarily equal, nor do they offer goods and services that objectively or subjectively match their respective social positions. This legal reciprocity is binding not only horizontally but also vertically. If an officer gives a soldier an order, the soldier has a duty to obey the order, whereas the officer has a duty to issue the order. Alternatively, the officer has a right to expect that his/her order will be fulfilled, and the soldier has a right to expect that the officer will not avoid issuing such an order.

Most importantly, the law in totalitarian countries not only has many sociopsychological implications, but it also affects the very essence of the theoretical understanding of the law. The correspondence between respective duties and rights is, in these systems, questionable. In each case, whether it is a simple relation between two parties or whether it is an interrelation between two corporate agencies located on different levels of the administrative hierarchy, corresponding rights and duties are only conditionally valid. At all times, a higher, publicly unknown metanorm may intervene and change altogether the content of the law vis-à-vis the respective parties (affecting, for example, contracts between partners or relations between subordinates). Political decisions may at any time transform all possible legal bonds. Thus, in totalitarian sociolegal systems, each norm has only suspended and conditional validity. The structure of the norm is not "A has a duty toward B; B has a duty toward A; whereas A has a right toward B, and B has a right toward A." Rather, the structure of the norm is that these interrelations are binding unless they are suspended or invalidated by the very structure of the quasi-legal metanorm, with its conditional character.

One might argue that in the era of *glasnost* and *perestroika*, post-totalitarian legal systems of the Soviet type, due to their more or less democratic ways of passing laws, have departed from the description presented above. But this argument does not hold. The laws, in some instances, are indeed enacted in a more open way, but the totalitarian-bureaucratic machinery that reinforces them still seems to operate in the same manner. In May 1989, a Polish-American team conducted a sociological study concerning *nomenklatura*, after the round table discussions between Polish dissidents and government that preceded the abolishment of communism. The team presented the following results: "How social policy would be pursued depends, to a large extent, on the apparatus of the government bureaucracy. But this, clearly, is not willing to yield to public pressure." And, "Polish bureaucracy does not support the Reform. This bureaucracy does not believe in the system, and it does not believe in itself" (Curry and Wasilewski 1989: 7).

But it is not just the Soviet brand of totalitarianism that seems to be dormant. A survey on fascism conducted in the seventies pointed out:

> For varying reasons hardly any of the men we interviewed thought that the "classical" forms of Fascism and Nazism still have any importance as alternative forms of government; most of them, however, were convinced that, given "certain conditions," there might be a "return" of Fascism or Nazism in an unforeseeable form, which would, however, be easily identifiable because of its resemblance to the prototypes. To us it seemed that only a few of these opinions revealed any awareness of the fact that, although right-wing solutions of the older type are hypothetically possible, the reactionary elements in general are tending—as Vittorio Foa succinctly put it—to move other pawns. This is also our own conclusion (Del Boca and Giovana 1970: 447).

This stigma of totalitarianism attaches laws to its conditional character and suspends them when it considers it expedient to do so. This is why sociolegal analysis is essential: analyzing the law without taking into consideration the social mechanisms and processes that transform it into social reality is too abstract. At the same time, analysis that tries to grasp the essential features of the social operation of the law is entirely misleading when limited to the question of the normative validity of the law.

The essence of the functioning of law under totalitarian systems is that the validity of each legal norm is deprived of any autonomy and depends entirely on the political content and sociopolitical practices that influence the norm. While on the surface the rule of law is respected in post-totalitarian systems, in reality, deeply entrenched organizational machinery remains in place. Furthermore, the values, mores, habits, and basic mechanisms generated under the totalitarian system still predominate. This post-totalitarian subculture deprives the new legal norms of their autonomy in an inconspicuous but potentially vicious way. In short: totalitarianism produces vestiges that do not quickly wither away.

The theory of totalitarianism formulated by Friedrich and Brzezinski stresses mainly the decisiveness of political factors in shaping the structure and inherent processes of totalitarian society. Nonetheless this theory does not show clearly the functionality of totalitarianism in repressing the accumulated political, social, and economic conflicts that divide totalitarian societies. The theory of communist totalitarianism developed by Łoś, on the other hand, accentuates economic factors and their inseparability from political processes. She singles out four stages of transformation in Marxist totalitarianism: (1) the stage of radical transformation; (2) the monopolistic stage; (3) the reformist stage; and (4) the stage of post-reformist decadence. The first stage is distinguished by a high level of national mobilization, attempts at a crash industrialization or radical reconstruction of the economy, intensive class struggle, vigilantism, likely mass movements of the population (for example, from countryside to the cities, forced resettlements of politically distrusted ethnic groups, and so forth) (Łoś 1990: 200).

The second stage is characterized by

the growing monopolistic tendencies of the party-state, expansion of the bureaucracy and of the central planning system, a tendency to create very large economic conglomerates, and either further reduction of the private sector or its greater regulation and coordination with the planned economy (Łoś 1990: 203).

Inevitably, by outlawing a vast range of economic activity, the monopolistic state enlarges the realm of the unofficial economy. The third stage is described in the following way:

When the period of industrial mobilization and reconstruction is over, the question of low productivity and its organizational causes comes to the fore. The party leadership's realization of the intrinsic limitations of the centralized economy is likely to prompt two types of reform that attempt to introduce certain elements of market: (1) internal reforms of the state economy and/or (2) a partial legitimization of the second economy (Łoś 1990: 214).

And the final stage:

Typical for this stage, a forced marriage of the state- and market-economies not only heightens their respective intrinsic contradictions, but also triggers attempts on the part of each economy to exploit the other in a largely parasitic, politicised and economically non-competitive manner (Łoś 1990: 219).

This last stage is crucial to the Communist party's realization of its own impotence and isolation. With the state economy in ruins, and the second economy expanding uncomfortably, the party's main source of power—its monopoly over the economy—becomes a patent fiction. Łoś's theory, developed in 1987, has been affirmed by the recent avalanche of changes in Central Europe. While it recognizes the importance of political processes, it sees them acting in concurrence with economic transformation. And since the whole system has been built on an assumption of the supremacy of the economy, the theory acknowledges the unique role the latter plays in the process of historical development and the decline of communist totalitarianism. This bolsters the point that totalitarianism requires a multidimensional approach if it is to be adequately explained.

Independently of political oppression, which is unique to totalitarian sociolegal systems, these systems generate a constant state of insecurity, anxiety, and vulnerability. This psychosocial state of affairs gives those who are on one side of the hidden sociopolitical conflict still better opportunities to use oppression against those who are governed. The macrosocial laboratory that furnished the history of humankind with the political experiences of three unforgettable years (1989, 1990, and 1991) additionally gave, as an unexpected by-product of these sociopolitical changes, a chance to watch *in vivo* the specificity of newly emerging post-totalitarian societies. The Polish case, which came first historically and was well described by several participant observers and by the leaders of the opposition movement, is the most self-conscious and therefore most transparent example, and thus provides an excellent opportunity for observing macrohistory in the making.

Therefore, it would be useful to try to pull together various observations relevant to this history as it is being made and attempt to describe the emergence of a new, post-totalitarian type of oppression, even if sufficient historical perspective is still lacking.

It should be noted that the history of humankind has produced various versions of totalitarianism. According to historical evidence, however, the communist type appears not only as oppressive, but as the most oppressive. Indeed, some authors claim that Western totalitarianism is subtly camouflaged as benevolent and directed not so much against individuals, but against the structure of social relationships through which they interact. This is the point made by Marcuse in his well-known book, *One-Dimensional Man*. Nonetheless, this point of view is presented in a more sophisticated way by Riesman. In the conclusion of his no-less-well-known work, *The Lonely Crowd*, he says:

> If the other-directed [the typical character of the "new" middle class—the bureaucrat, the salaried employee in business, etc.; what is common to all the other-directed people is that their contemporaries are the source of direction for the individual] people should discover how much needless work they do, discover that their own thoughts and their own lives are quite as interesting as other people's, that, indeed, they no more assuage their loneliness in a crowd of peers than one can assuage one's thirst by drinking sea water, then we might expect them to become more attentive to their own feelings and aspirations (Riesman 1961: 307).

Using Poland as a case study, the next chapter will look at a concrete social system that tries to liberate itself from latent political conflicts, legal restrictions, cognitive limitations, erstwhile attitudinal habits, and the effects of emotional pains. Polish society was the first in the Soviet bloc to reject the yoke of totalitarianism and trigger the large wave of antitotalitarian uprisings in other countries. It therefore seems to be the most suitable target for an analysis of the social forces unleashed by prolonged systemic pressure, and of the unique totalitarian heritage that subsequently bestows oppression upon those who have been fighting against it. The analysis should show more clearly those persistent types of unexpected by-products implanted into social life by the former organizational system based on structured oppression.

NOTES

1. Basic principles of Bolshevik *Weltanschauung* are:

(a) the demand for complete and unqualified loyalty to the Party; (b) the insistence on the necessary conflict of interests between the working class of which the Party is the leader and all other classes and the need for unrelenting conflict against these other classes, even in times of apparent truce and cooperation; (c) the continuous application of the criteria of Party interests in judging every person and situation and the need to avoid eclecticism in doctrine and opportunism and compromise in practice; (d) the stress on the class characteristics of individuals and the interpretation of their actions in the light of their class position exclusively; (e) the belief that all history is the history of class conflict; (f) the denial of the existence of pure truth and attack on those who espouse pure science or "art for art's sake"; (g) the belief that the expression of sentiment is an expression of weakness and that it interferes with the correct interpretation of reality and the choice of the right course of action; (h) the belief in the ubiquitousness of the influence of "Wall Street," the "City," the "Big Banks," "Heavy Industry," "200 Families," etc. and their masked control over even the most remote spheres of life and the counterbelief in the necessity to penetrate organizations and achieve complete control over them; (i) the ideal of the classless society, without private property in the instruments of production and hence without conflict, the "realm of freedom" where man will cease his alienation and become truly human (Shils in Mason 1967: 33).

2. My information on the Polish judiciary comes mainly from my experience as a practicing lawyer (legal counsel) from 1952–1956. (See also Grzeskowiak 1989: 4.)

3. In 1990 Gorbachev went through a heavy battle to liquidate this constitutional fiction. In 1991 the concept of "Soviet Union" was liquidated. Several new states emerged; among them Russia, Ukraine, and Belarus. The influence of Gorbachev and those forces that operated behind him should not be underestimated.

5

A Concise Theory of Post-Totalitarian Oppression

It is well known that the father of totalitarian phraseology was Mussolini. His charismatic qualities, which many people found irresistible, gave totalitarianism its initial meaning. This meaning was transformed completely, however, and the political and social applications of totalitarianism led to its condemnation. Totalitarianism was also censured on scientific grounds thanks to Hannah Arendt's scholarly determination (Arendt 1962). Nevertheless, in both the initial phase (the phase of glory) and the later phase (unanimous condemnation), the dominance of ideology over political, social, and economic life was a constant factor. Szczepański (1990: 7–8) goes straight to the heart of totalitarianism:

> Totalitarianism is frequently confused with other forms of authoritarian power—military dictatorship or primitive tyranny. The latter two are notorious for their naked and brutal violence, but they lack the most dangerous element of totalitarianism, i.e., a monopolistic ideology. It is this ideology, irrespective of its specific orientation, which lies at the roots of totalitarian coercion. It prohibits all opposition and discussion and puts all the power in the hands of one, usually minority, party. This party creates the fiction of the "will of the people" and monopolizes public opinion by taking over the mass media. It provides the exclusive patterns of education, makes the decisions about the forms of culture and social

relationships and everything that constitutes the domain of free and creative human will. And finally, it inevitably transforms into a power system led by the hierarchic and privileged party oligarchy which holds onto its power by means of a ramified bureaucracy and police.

It is not surprising that the first comprehensive insight comes from a German scholar. Franz Neumann in 1957 (1957: 245) described totalitarianism in this way:

The control of society, now as important as the control of the state, is achieved by the following techniques:

1. The leadership principle - to enforce guidance from the top and responsibility to the top.
2. The "synchronization" of all social organizations - not only to control them, but to make them serviceable to the state.
3. The creation of graded elites - so as to enable the rulers to control the masses from within and to disguise manipulation from without, for example, to supplement bureaucracies in the narrow meaning of the term with private leadership groups within the various strata of the population.
4. The atomization and isolation of the individual, which involves negatively the destruction or at least weakening of social units based on biology (family), tradition, religion, or co-operation in differentiated mass organizations which leave the individual isolated and more easily manipulable.
5. The transformation of culture into propaganda - of cultural values into saleable commodities.

The final factor in totalitarianism is the reliance upon terror, that is, the use of non-calculable violence as a permanent threat against the individual.

WHAT IS POST-TOTALITARIANISM?

Marxism, in its all-confusing analyses, pertinaciously (or stubbornly) suggested that liberal-capitalist societies, with their alleged overpowering and oppressive nature (which acts invisibly, in a deceitful and mendacious way), are essentially even more totalitarian. With this formulation, Marxism was able to avoid, for awhile, any academic or public analysis of the problem. The spectacular fall of Marxism in 1989, initiated by the activity of Polish *Solidarnosc*, brought the problem dramatically to the fore once again. When Marxism collapsed along with its purely totalitarian political creations, however, post-totalitarianism became the more interesting issue.

In his book on the post-totalitarian system, Goldfarb quotes the opinions of several Polish intellectuals (Baranczak, Michnik, Staniszkis) with a journalistic flair. However, the only really interesting discussion of post-totalitarianism is to be found in the words of the Czech playwright and president, Vaclav Havel:

Between the aims of the post-totalitarian system and the aims of life there is a yawning abyss: while life, in the essence, moves towards plurality, diversity, independent self-constitution and self-organization, in short, towards fulfilment of its own freedom, the post-totalitarian system demands conformity, uniformity, and discipline. While life ever strives to create new and "improbable" structures, the post-totalitarian system contrives to force life into its most probable states (Havel in Goldfarb 1989: 106-7).

Post-totalitarianism is a socioeconomic system that pretends to be politically and culturally pluralistic, but organizationally and socially, it is still a cohesive outcome of the long-standing reign of authoritarian regime. In other words, it is a system that, though free of the overt political forms of totalitarianism, is nonetheless affected by the social structures typical of totalitarianism.

Does closer scrutiny support these generalizations? I shall attempt to show that it does by means of ten basic conditions, in each of which can be seen the vestigial, and sometimes paradoxical, influence of totalitarianism upon its successor. The conditions are as follows:

1. the continued existence of a *nomenklatura* (people appointed to executive posts on the basis of the party's tested membership), its continued functioning based on a "soft landing" after the fall of totalitarianism, and the cohabitation of two opposing *nomenklatura*, old and new;

2. increased social frustration because specific categories of people have not been brought to account for their actions; society demands that people be held accountable for their past collaboration with the totalitarian system; accountability is demanded not on the basis of personal complaints but on the basis of an objective assessment of the nature of a person's participation in state affairs. Society also demands that people who held higher posts in the party and state administration be banned from the state administration.

3. perpetuation of a bureaucracy of "expertise," which grew out of the systematic liquidation of the traditional intelligentsia and the parallel, systematic creation and expansion of the technological-administrative type of "intelligentsia";

4. continued and constant influence on social life of the authoritarian official legal system and its attendant customs;

5. continued ownership by the state of basic institutions and enterprises, because the call for "privatization" does not change, by fiat, the existing state of affairs;

6. the continued functioning of customs formed in the period of systematic and intensive "sovietization," due both to inertia and to the continued social utility of these customs;

7. unconstrained development of clerical and dogmatic-religious modes

of thinking (which previously served to counterbalance the political totalitarianism);

8. the systematic disappearance of the once-prevalent central steering of social, cultural, and economic processes, based on abstract principles;

9. the low level of development of democratic institutions in Poland (One must learn how to be free. One must respect compromise, be aware of the limits to acceptable polemic, and of the shortcomings of forcing one's own point of view. Various democratically established modes of social dialogue must be worked out. These include selection of administration, the principles underlying public discussion, the promotion of impartiality in thinking about social issues and in social practice, liquidation of the effects of "false awareness," elimination of various forms of "sham activities," and so on.);

10. the continued enslavement of the "social mentality"; one must become aware of the "thought muzzles" forced onto official and lay modes of thinking by almost half a century of systematic Marxist training systems.

EXPOSITION OF THE TEN POSTULATES

The *Nomenklatura*

We know that the *nomenklatura* is a social stratum consisting of higher state and party officials, individually preselected and approved by the central committee of the political party currently in power. In those countries where "real" socialism reigned, this stratum formed the basic executive apparatus of the communist system. People were selected to the nomenklatura not on the basis of professional competence and practical experience but on the basis of their predetermined political loyalty toward the central party organs and, at times, toward specific party leaders.

When real socialism collapsed, this stratum retained its power because (1) it knew how to find the ropes in the tangle it had made of state organizations and institutions of its own devising; (2) it manifested a considerable degree of conformity toward the new administration; (3) it had learned, over the years in office, to cleverly expose those vivid justifications or rationalizations that proved expedient at any given time; and (4) it still had a monopoly over many secret elements of administrative functioning. For these reasons, some people believe that keeping the nomenklatura in office is relatively innocuous or even, at times, beneficial, in light of other urgent economic and political priorities.

The nomenklatura made use of the initial post-totalitarian period of uncertainty over its fate to draw on those potentials to which it had direct practical access. So, when the call for privatization was launched, it immediately and noiselessly took hold of the key posts in the new companies. Despite the fact that the members of the ex-nomenklatura were now without political power, they were able, due to their instrumental abilities, to gain easy access to economic comfort by getting hold of lucrative posts in the new economic enterprises: the "soft-landing" strategy. One such case of blatant safeguarding involves the Polish-German Gromada Tourist Company, which intends to convert the tourist-class Farmers' Inn into a luxury hotel. The person in charge of Berlin capital in Warsaw is General Straszewski, who was formerly at the Ministry of Internal Affairs and is now vice chairman of the company (Fredro-Boniecki 1990: 89).

The old nomenklatura has easily given way to the new one. Although there have been many loud protests against any insinuation that a new nomenklatura has formed and is taking the place of or coexisting with the old one, observations of how people are being selected for executive posts, the existence of a "drawing-room" (selecting committees that accept those who belong), and the tendency to select higher executives brought up in these drawing-rooms suggest that personal factors and even cliquishness, not objective performance standards, are at the base of key promotions. Morally, of course, the new nomenklatura differs fundamentally from the old. The new one is basically determined, first and foremost, to undo all the wrongs previously implemented on the basis of the "dirty togetherness" principle—that is, the principle of reciprocity according to which one could, or even should, use one's official position to arrange private matters for oneself, one's family, and—most important—for those who would later reciprocate with similar favors. The most prominent feature of this partnership is that, though illegal, it leads to social cohesion due to the continuous threat of blackmail through exposure of the beneficiary of the partnership. The new nomenklatura firmly discards the "dirty togetherness" principle. It bases its activities on decency and accountability for one's actions.

Both nomenklatures act within a specific symbiosis: the old one does not fully denounce the new (although it has access to old documents that it could make use of—allegedly every eighth citizen in what used to be the German Democratic Republic collaborated with the secret police). The new one does not eliminate the old (which works reliably for the new one). This symbiosis, though conducive to the smooth functioning of the social system as a whole, is harmful enough to lead to internal stagnation. One may even predict that this specific alliance will begin to work for the benefit of both the old and the new nomenklatura when the new one comes under threat. One may also foresee that the new nomenklatura will then gain the absolute approval of the old one, because the only safeguard for the old nomenklatura is the new one. History sometimes plays strange pranks. The hangman and the victim need each other: the hangman needs the victim in order to save his/her skin, the victim needs the hangman so as not to lose his/her newly gained privileges. However one looks at it, one can see clearly the co-existence of opposing forces that both fight and support each other.

Accountability

The new nomenklatura adopted the principle of not holding the old nomenklatura responsible for its actions. At a time when the country must be built economically and politically; when the new and still in-experienced administration ("one must learn politics as one learns to ride a bike!") confronts the problem of sweeping away the bad inter-personal relations left by "real socialism"; and given the problem of exchanging the previous evil with a new, healthy, and rational relation-ship (as demanded by the new "middle class") or Christian relationships (as demanded by the majority of society and by the victorious Church hierarchy)—then to immediately hold people responsible for their ac-tions could prove to be a menace, sabotaging moral reconstruction on a global scale.

Half a century of human frustration requires compensation, however. This is a task within the sphere of social reality. How, then, does one discharge accumulated, justified frustration without unleashing a mob-bish desire for the immediate hanging of the guilty (and at times also the suspect) from street lamps? A draft proposal concerning the political reform of the state was prepared in 1982 and later disseminated in closed circles (the weekly *Tygodnik Powszechny* refused to publish it in 1990 because its ideas were supposedly out of date). The proposal held that

> the federation should forbid the holding of any state post by ex-members of the administrative elite who held higher posts in the state administra-tion. Those who led to harm through their criminal activities can regain their right to speak in public when they actively work on behalf of an-nulling the harm of their own doing. Persons who held *nomenklatura* po-sitions should be brought before Desovietization Committees (equivalent to the denazification Committees) and should be treated in accordance with the decisions of these committees (Podgórecki 1982: 10).

The basic idea was to treat the process of desovietization impersonally and to avoid claims for compensation for personal wrongs. Instead, certain categories of people were to be punished for a given type of activity and, thus, for implementing a regime with criminal outcomes. The target of punishment was to be an objective category of people, not individuals. Of course, criminal behavior of specific people would be treated individually.

This policy aimed at instilling in human consciousness not only personal responsibility but also responsibility for the behavior of specific social categories of people. The practice of justice along these lines would allow the discharge of frustration but would also help to avoid a witch hunt. Moreover, it would teach a lesson to those responsible for social wrongs, whereby wrongs should be undone with one's own hands. Again, one finds here certain opposing currents.

Bureaucracy of "Expertise"

One of the characteristic features of totalitarianism, especially in Poland, was the systematic destruction of the traditional intelligentsia as a separate social stratum. In Poland and Russia (and, to a certain extent, in Hungary), the intelligentsia regarded acting for the benefit of its own society, country, or nation as its basic duty. It did not pursue its own welfare (Gella 1989). In fact, one unique feature of this stratum was its conviction that its mission was to provide education and social services to the "lower" strata. Another unique characteristic of the intelligentsia was its heroic pursuit of independence. "Sovietization" systematically strove to eliminate this idea from the social conscience and to replace it with the ideology of the "working intelligentsia," a social stratum with higher technical or administrative (but not humanistic) education. The ideology of the new social category—the working intelligentsia—focused on providing the government in office with up-to-date reports on the state of society (Konrad and Szelényi 1979). That the "socialization" of this stratum had been successful became evident when part of it, members of the *nomenklatura*, noiselessly crossed over to the victorious Solidarity.

Thus, one of the unique features of totalitarianism was its ability to call to life, in a relatively short time, a new social stratum that was completely lacking in ideals, ready to serve anybody who had power, and willing to operate as a new *salariat*. The civil service and bureaucracy (in Weber's impersonal sense) familiar to the West did not emerge in Poland from the bourgeoisie but were recruited from an upwardly mobile peasantry and people from small towns. These people owed their rise, which was not so much material as social (in an illusory sense), to the new administration. Since they were alienated from the customs of the traditional intelligentsia, however, they were at the disposal of the current orders of the centers of power. Their readiness to obey orders provided the foundation for a new type of social loyalty—loyalty toward the "commies." This civil servant and technocratic intelligentsia, formed during the period of Stalinist totalitarianism, rolled inertly into post-totalitarianism. However, the "expertise" of this social category resembled the drunkard's lamppost: it did not illuminate the surroundings but merely served as a leaning post. Again, we have the clash of *sui generis* opposing currents: the ghost ideology of the remainders of the traditional intelligentsia demanded nonegocentric activity, whereas the new ideology of the administrative and technological "experts" remains servile. It is this administrative-expert stratum that is responsible for the state of the law in Poland. The law formulated by these administrative "specialists" led to such absurdities as the Presidium of the Government settling the wages of cleaning women and the Ministry of Finance determining the operations for filleting and salting fish (Podgórecki 1957: 3).

Influence of the Legal System on Social Life

Social life was dominated by the repressive, inquisitorial nature of official laws, which also penetrated osmotically into civil law. The call for law and order was, in fact, the call for law to cover up reality, which, in itself, was anything but law-abiding. *Intuitive* law (i.e., the law invoked by two trustworthy partners with a joint reason for keeping up their trustworthiness) was constantly eroded by the bureaucratic degeneration of the law (Podgórecki et al., forthcoming). The post-totalitarian social and legal systems confront lawyers with the extremely difficult and intellectually unrewarding task of weeding out the remnants of the previous legal inflation. Lawyers have the task of getting rid of the effects of inconsistency in the hierarchies of validity of legal acts, and the task of finding a way to disentangle the illogical and nonsensical, normative constructions elaborated within the unruliness of theoretical Marxism. Post-totalitarian lawyers must also see to it that the new, sensible legal acts are consistent with the old ones that, though faulty, are still in force. Again, one may notice here the presence of two opposing streams.

Continued State Ownership

In the post-totalitarian phase, the state still owns the basic economic spheres—the railways, mining and chemical industries, shipbuilding, the military, the so-called heavy and textile industries, the banks (though new private banks are now beginning to open), science (including the universities, the Polish Academy of Sciences, and many research institutes), the core of the mass media and publishing houses—to name only the most important branches of life directly or indirectly related to the economy. All these branches are subordinated to public law, that is, law as formulated during the totalitarian period. And once again, one can see the mark of the old on the new system in a rigid structure of property based on the public law of the impersonal state juxtaposed with rapidly developing private enterprises. True, this structure is crumbling here and there thanks to various trends toward privatization (introduced earlier in the form of joint-stock companies, mainly established by the old *nomenklatura* in the process of changing its skin). The situation remains basically unchanged, however.

Totalitarian Customs

Due to inertia, many patterns of behavior elaborated during the period of systematic sovietization of the country are still in force. They appear in different areas of life and take numerous forms, of which the basic ones are "dirty togetherness," the tendency to set up claims, and instrumentalism.

"Dirty togetherness," as described earlier, functions not only in those social areas where it was directly established (such as in what has been identified in Russia as the *krugovaja poruka*, or circular assurance). Each existing sphere of "dirty togetherness" has the potential to seek out additional connections with similar partnerships. "Dirty togetherness" draws on the institution called "access" (Wedel 1986). If a given demand does not lie within the practical possibilities of a usual partner, he/she may involve others by means of help of his/her own partners. This is because totalitarian societies and, to an even greater extent, post-totalitarian societies, function on the basis of a general matrix of different, more or less interconnected partnerships. Just as the "second economy" supplements or eats into the state economy (Łoś 1990), so also "dirty togetherness" is a hidden reality that corrects or modifies all manifest social processes. Another specific feature of this reality is that it makes use of all formal and official structures in order to take them over for private goals, taking advantage of their administrative potential and formal power. Things that cannot be arranged legally and officially are arranged through a chain of connections: private—official—private. Of course, the pool of official positive decisions is limited, so "dirty togetherness" uses its private connections to take over part of this pool for itself, leaving less for official procedures, and sometimes it takes over the entire pool.

Another side effect of the sovietization of Polish society is the tendency to set up claims. Everybody, whether or not they have legal justification, demands from others (institutions, organizations, and the state) what they can claim. These claims may be related to their most basic needs but they can also be quite esoteric; they are unusually excessive. By making such claims, people are not just trying to be visible. When contending with each other over justified demands, it is important that they be dynamic and aggressive in the process. People believe that if they demand a lot they will receive at least part of what they want. This general atmosphere of claiming is less obvious inside the country. Everybody is claiming something, so there is little variation in styles of behavior. It is when one leaves the country that the differences become striking. Polish emigrants who appear on various European and non-European scenes, especially in Australia, Canada, and West Germany (Zawadzka 1991) differ in the intensity of their claims, but they are always rapacious. Nevertheless, the following generalization is suggested: the later someone left the country (i.e., the longer his or her experience of sovietization), the more intense the claims.

Instrumentality is the most general product of sovietization. Since survival itself becomes a problem, not to mention decent survival, one ought to grasp at all possible means of guaranteeing survival, according to the canons of social experience. And any means leading to this goal are acceptable. By this reckoning, the imperative of the traditional intelligentsia to serve its own society becomes almost absurd. Such concepts as patriotism, fatherland, and social service (the last one was additionally ridiculed and devalued by the Stalinist demand for "social action") very soon become empty. The important thing is an individual's own business, which is frequently understood to mean the welfare of one's own children, which is actually one's own business too. When we guarantee our children comforts that we did not have ourselves, we aim at compensating for our own deprivations. The totalitarian VIPs and various "official" patriots sent their grown-up children abroad. This, of course, required careful, instrumental preparation.

These various customs, born under the pressure of an alien, enforced totalitarian ideology, were completely functional when they were used in self-defense. In the post-totalitarian period, they still have considerable utilitarian potential. They still live on (autotelically) and function autonomously, despite the fact that political oppression no longer exists. There are undoubtedly several reasons why this is so, but two seem predominant. First of all, instrumentalism is a universal worldwide trend nowadays. It is particularly conspicuous in American, German, and Japanese youth as well as in young Jews who have undergone many years of communization in Soviet Russia. It is also found in the young Chinese. Second, the idea of the traditional Polish intelligentsia was undoubtedly a great burden. Once discarded, it gives way to a feeling of considerable personal freedom. In view of the lack of clear ideals and values that could give cohesion to society as a whole (with the exception of negative ideals such as opposition to communism), the strategy of seeking ways to survive on one's own seems more attractive.

Leon Petrazycki spoke of "psychological venoms" (Petrażycki 1985: 239–41), and these were particularly evident under the totalitarian regime. Suspicion of neighbors, family, or sometimes even one's own children; instrumental and altruistic denunciations; erosion of friendships; administrative corruption; "dirty togetherness"; the systematic transformation of traditionally respected linguistic symbols into negative slogans (e.g., democracy); generalized fear; reluctance to speak the truth; constant self-censorship—these are some of the venoms. They cannot be wiped out within a few days. In the post-totalitarian era, they become autonomized and continue to live on as an "internal-negative automatic force."

It may be assumed that the mental heritage of the totalitarian era is like a miasma hovering in wait, ready to enfold at any moment, and with increased force, a society engaged in the process of psychic rebirth.

Clericalism and Religion

One of the reasons why totalitarianism broke down was that it was opposed by traditional Polish Catholicism. This Catholicism is connected to various, sometimes obscure patriotic attitudes and it proved to be a persistent adversary, tempered by its centuries-old quest for survival. One side effect of the overthrow of totalitarianism and the victory of religiousness was unexpectedly widespread clericalism (an increased feeling of power in Church authorities, leading to the spread of pride in the overthrow of totalitarianism, the martyrdom of several Polish priests, and the charisma of the Polish pope to all representatives of the Church). The sudden boost in clerical self-esteem has not been accompanied by an intellectual deepening of Christian doctrine (nothing new has appeared here except the reception of French personalism and isolated phenomenological discussions). Catholic dogma has tended to become not only ideologically but also practically more rigid. The complete intimidation of the Polish senate during the 1991 vote on the antiabortion bill is a conspicuous example.

The mere receding of totalitarianism does not guarantee the parallel systematic development of tolerance or the cultivation of a pluralistic outlook, but it is connected, paradoxically, with the reinforcement of a different totalitarian outlook. Maybe it sounds blasphemous to compare fascist or communist totalitarianism with Catholic totalitarianism; however, the comparison is not aimed at the criminal practices of the former and the patriotic-prosocial outcomes of the latter but at their similar mentality: In one as in the other, everything is subordinated to another all-encompassing ideology. After almost complete incapacitation by criminal totalitarianism, society stands before a trap—the cul-de-sac of gratitude for the authoritarian savior.

Nevertheless, it is worth noting that the *nomenklatura* has not withdrawn completely into a defensive position. There are some persistent (although not easily verifiable) indications of well-planned and well-executed anti-Church action on its part; in certain morally and politically controversial areas, there are clear signs of a disinformation campaign. For instance, highly repressive opinions regarding abortion and other related matters (such as family planning) have been attributed to the Church, which the Church—due to its principled stance—is not willing to denounce. A careful reading of official Church pronouncements shows that the Polish Church leaders' stand on these controversial matters has been quite reasonable and restrained. Contrary to general belief, they have not lent their support to a highly punitive anti-abortion bill that so largely preoccupied the lower body of the Polish parliament (The Diet) in 1991. The image of the Church appears to have been manipulated, and there are signs that a quasi-alliance of former security forces, some ex-communist party activists, and anti-Church leftist circles has been responsible.

Central Steering

Thinking in macrosocial categories falls to pieces in the era of post-totalitarianism; however, no new political doctrine takes its place automatically. People are reluctant to acknowledge that there is no one, synthetic, true philosophy of thought and action. They yearn for a general truth. Since none appears immediately, things backfire and people begin to turn once again to party "gods" of the previous era, who have, meanwhile, changed into Western clothes. Hence, the comeback of Z. Bauman or L. Kołakowski (the latter, previously an outspoken enemy of Catholicism, now gives a hermeneutic lesson on how to understand Christianity to the chief editor of the catholic weekly *Tygodnik Powszechny*). Therefore, under post-totalitarianism, freedom and truth can appear alternately as mulch for the still-totalitarian garden.

Development of Democratic Institutions

One must learn how to be free. Recently, a series of prestigious lectures given by leading Polish intellectuals was held in the capital of a Western European country. After one lecture, the speaker was asked which Western institutions he thought could be transferred to Poland to help the country in its democratic reconstruction. The speaker blushed with joy and said:

> I've thought a lot about this. I always repeat the same thing in such cases. We must apply a three-in-one system. The first element is cognition. Then we must add a second element—the development of adequate abilities. Cognition and abilities must be supplemented by attitude modelling. Then the three-in-one system will begin to function. And it can be fully utilized for democracy.

Abstract, Marxist, all-encompassing rubbish gives birth, through its osmotic, persistent, cultivated implantation, to another type of bastard. The sense of every utterance is verified at the appropriate level of generalization. If freedom is to consist in feeding the hungry with abstract gibberish, people may come to yearn for the Stalinist whip. That, at least, gives a straightforward answer.

In Poland, there is no orderly and systematic information about how people are selected for specific posts. It would be difficult to believe, however, that the last remaining human feeling on the road to the Communist Heaven—logrolling—could be eliminated immediately. However, this procedure could be limited quite drastically by the widespread introduction of competitions. Even seconding, that simple mechanism of parliamentary discussion, is unknown in Poland. There is not even an appropriate term in Polish for this practice.

It is essential to hammer home the sense of impersonal procedures in a society polluted with "dirty togetherness" and favoritism. It is also important to unmask various concepts in the sphere of Marxist false awareness, to excavate with archaeological precision the true values and meanings of concepts, and to eliminate myths ruthlessly, not only myths pertaining to various scientific or pseudoscientific conceptions but also legends about particular people that are particularly widely disseminated. It is noteworthy that in the era of totalitarianism, when censorship enforced silence, the same voices were heard again and again; they were imprinted in public consciousness by the media of party propaganda. Why, in post-totalitarianism, do we still persistently hear the same voices, although they now declare ideas that contradict their own previous opinions? Have they made the effort to compensate for the now-obvious harm they once did? And where are those who carried the burden of supervision and kept alive the values of a civil society? Are they all gone? Who notices that those whose names were not made public by the negative propaganda of Stalinist totalitarianism are banished to the realm of civic nonexistence? Not everybody joined the disciplined lines of the embattled Solidarity.

Totalitarianism encouraged people to take up "sham activity" and at the same time to defend themselves against its consequences. The post-totalitarian period is also laden with sham activities (maniacal rummaging through personal data and empty disputes; avoiding any declaration of political programs; covering up ignorance as to economic matters on a broader scale; celebrating various religious feast days and patriotic anniversaries; waiting for help from the West, etc.), though their content and goals are different. Post-totalitarianism tends to inhibit spontaneity in order to counteract sham activity, but at the same time it shuts off the potential for a real search for new ways. Thus, a new network of opposing currents surfaces. Sham activities block the way for authentic

activity in the totalitarian system, whereas in post-totalitarianism, authentic activity is inhibited in order to counteract sham activities.

Thought Muzzles

Post-totalitarianism has the prerequisites for discarding the "thought
muzzles" of totalitarianism. However, the existential experiences of a
threefold loss of independence and a fourfold change of sociopolitical
system were unable to stimulate the literary and scientific description
of these mutations, unique in the history of humankind. Is it not de-
plorable, in such a case, to expect inspiration from the West or to copy
its fads? During the war, life proceeded in make-believe fashion. Does
it not proceed nowadays dictated by the plebbish instincts?

CONCLUSIONS

In a totalitarian system, economy is subordinated to politics; however,
this political supremacy covers relatively short periods of time. Totalitarianism is unique in that social and economic structure of totalitarian
social systems is determined directly by the accessibility to political
power. The closer one is placed to the center of power, the more he/she
enjoys political privileges (which usually are strictly connected with the
distribution of economic goods); the more someone is transferred toward
the periphery of political power, the lower is his/her life pushed below
the subsistence level. Post-totalitarian social systems demonstrate one
more paradox: although in these systems former monopolistic centers
of ideology and political power are disintegrated, previously dominant
social forces still decide, intentionally or by inertia, the distribution of
goods or services as they did under the totalitarian regimes. Havel (1992:
1–2) corroborates this point saying,

> The authoritarian regime imposed a certain order (and doing so "legitim-
> ized" them, in a sense). This order has now been shattered, but a new
> order that would limit rather than exploit these views, an order based on
> freely accepted responsibility to and for the whole society, has not yet
> been built - nor could it have been, for such an order takes years to develop
> and cultivate. Thus we are witnesses to a bizarre state of affairs: society
> has freed itself, true, but in some ways it behaves worse than when it was
> in chains.

It is the material status of the people that is the decisive factor in the
long run. But not the status determined by ownership (real or ostensible)
of the means of production; what counts is having at one's disposal

material resources enabling the gratification of basic needs, including those needs that are dictated by the worldwide "revolution of demands."

Totalitarianism creates not only rigid, centrally controlled economic mutations but also a redundancy of legal regulations. It also establishes centers of social control that block the uncontrolled proliferation of sociocultural activity. What is more, the social structures created by the system continue to exist even when the political and ideological monolith of totalitarian power has ceased to exist.

The most enduring remnant of the totalitarian system is not only an efficient old *nomenklatura* transformed into a conformist quasi-private stratum but also thought habits and "psychological venoms," which, though externally intangible, penetrate everything.

The most characteristic feature of the post-totalitarian system is the dual current of social life. On the one hand, we have open, pluralistic political reforms, open public discussions, and liquidation of state censorship, and on the other hand, we find the internal censorship of the new, antitotalitarian totalitarianism and the lack of means or efficient "transmitters" capable of passing on the outcomes of public discussions to those centers that have real influence on social life. Finally, and most importantly, we have the systematic perpetuation of the social heritage of the totalitarian system.

The development of post-totalitarianism leads to new paradoxes. Although it may seem that thoughts are the most volatile, intangible, and mobile of things, many thought relics of totalitarianism have become so deeply imbedded in human minds that it is impossible to get rid of them or to formulate new ideas. One would think that now, at last, when totalitarianism has fallen, uprightness would become a widely respected virtue, and yet it is quite the opposite. Upright people are a challenge for others. It is better to keep them at bay, since everybody has something on his or her conscience. Since in the era of totalitarianism many things were settled once and for all whereas in post-totalitarianism many problems require creative and frequently tedious reflection, many people reveal nostalgia for the previous state of repressive order. In the end, the victims of totalitarianism must resign from their justified compensation because the inherited system is economically inefficient.

It is also worthy of note that in the post-totalitarian society the rule of law, which is invoked in order to establish foundations of justice and equality, works in an opposite direction. Paradoxically, it tends to aggravate the totalitarian inequality. The rule of law appears unable to fulfill its democratic function in a situation in which the framework of privileges generated by the totalitarian regime remains in place. Without its removal, the rule of law, which is supposed to treat everybody according to the law, contributes to the preservation of existing privileges, thus legitimizing social injustice. The formal neutrality of the law tends to petrify existing relations. Consequently, its democratic premises notwithstanding, the rule of law may give credibility and sanction to the unjustly acquired privileges.

The above discussion shows that social change in a post-totalitarian system is not directly contingent upon economic factors. These can play a significant part as immediate claims for improvement of the standard of living (through strikes, riots, peasant manifestations, etc.) or as channelled claims (demands concerning conditions of work, slogans modelled after the revolution of demands). In a totalitarian system, the means of production were formally owned, on the basis of constitutional law, by the "working class." In fact, however, they were owned by the *nomenklatura*, popularly known in Poland as the "owners of the Polish People's Republic." This ownership was based on intuitive (unwritten, practical, customary) law. Intuitive law is generally socially accepted though it is inconsistent with the official law. In this case, however, it was not accepted. The schizophrenic split of law and doctrine was well recognized by society and led to the rejection of any legitimization of the socialist system. Under totalitarianism the ownership of the means of production, contrary to the existing doctrine, had the significant economic consequences mentioned above. Under post-totalitarianism, it has taken on a new meaning—it has enabled privatization, that is, reification[1] of previously wielded power.

Under post-totalitarianism, the old political forces, now without power and always without legitimacy, are quite insignificant (although they have their hooks in certain branches of the social-control system), and they meet with explicit social condemnation. The new authorities have, at their highest level, widespread social approval. However, they are inefficient in the recruitment of higher-level administration because the executive authorities (1) are still partly on the side of the old apparatus; (2) have a shattered morale; (3) are cynical to a considerable extent; (4) are anti-impersonal; and (5) frequently obey orders merely out of a habit of conformity. The unconditional acceptance of the highest authorities springs from negation of the old regime and not from acceptance of the new program. These authorities do not have sufficient support and understanding at the lower levels of the administrative apparatus, however. Post-totalitarianism brings with it an ebullient state of social warpedness or crookedness—uncertainty about whether people, who are constantly dissociated, are responding predictably to typical social motivations, appeals, and incentives or whether they are reacting haphazardly and unpredictably. But in post-totalitarianism we also find a warped middle-level administration, that is, an administration basically formed under the totalitarian system. It is foreseeable that the new administration, based on the idea of "acceleration," will have to reckon not only with the remnants of totalitarianism and post-totalitarianism but also with several elements of the new *nomenklatura*, which, having only just got a taste of power, will be reluctant to lose it.[2]

Old monolithic outlooks will have a limited role in post-totalitarianism. The derivative-ideological role of the communist doctrine is well recognized. Catholicism, in turn, is beginning to limit its scope to celebrating rituals or else it is returning to its proper role as go-between in the eternal consolidation of the covenant with the suprahuman. The strength of the new, embryonic programs lies mainly in their destruction of previous outlooks.

"Social structures," as they are popularly (and intuitively) called, are a decisive factor in the present multidimensional kaleidoscope of factors. These structures, according to an earlier discussion, should be interpreted as consolidated social meta-attitudes. These attitudes, though invisible, are central among historically determined collective motivations, functioning with specific force and camouflaged inertia. Under the term meta-attitudes, one should understand those social sets that combine many other ordinary or mundane attitudes in a consistent whole. A specific configuration of meta-attitudes can be regarded as typical for Polish society: instrumentalism, survival, spectacular adherence to principles and podginess (confusion of authenticity and unintended pretense). Although these meta-attitudes appear in different historical-political and socioeconomic settings with varying force, they are the product of mutations that are characteristic of this society as a whole (Podgórecki 1976 and 1987).

In sum, the uniqueness of the post-totalitarian social system, as it manifested itself in Poland, can be summarized in the following way: the global, total, and unequivocal populist rejection of totalitarianism that culminated in 1989 and 1990 pushed the social forces, movements, and ideologies that had just entered public life in the opposite direction from the former communist trust. But since the opposite pole of the previously officially accepted options was still "occupied" by the "social void" (Podgórecki 1976; Nowak 1979), these emerging new post-totalitarian forces, movements, and ideologies tended to linger toward those tangible remainders that were, and are, still discernible. The overwhelming rejection of totalitarianism (with the exception of the small but relatively influential *nomenklatura*) as a sociopolitical system did not necessarily mean the rejection of those cognitive categories, behaviors, structural informal arrangements, and institutional and organizational schemes that have been created during the prolonged rule of the totalitarian regime. These patterns, although criticized and seemingly barren, persisted as the primary available schemes of public interactions. Thus, the main trust of the newly generated official life, was channelled through formerly valid patterns, to enter eventually into the territory of an entirely different authenticity. It belonged to the double-structured entity of a disparate epistemological order. From one point of view, this entity was (and is) concerned with eternal phenomena, but from the other point of view it was (and is) engaged in the guidance of those sociopolitical processes that take place *hic et nunc* (here and now).

This body, traditionally deeply rooted in national and social life, recently gained considerable sympathy when it engaged, despite its "destiny of a higher order" in an open war against the vicious, frontal, and manipulative assaults of totalitarianism. Clearly, such war was impossible to win. In persistent battles, fiscal pressures, administrative measures, physical terror, and repetitive persuasions have been used against defenseless normative solicitations and appeals. This body, was, of course, represented by the Polish Catholic Church. Its main goal was to remind the overwhelming majority of the population that zero hour would inevitably arrive. Under the regime of totalitarianism, nobody expected that it would come so soon, and that the Church would become, surprisingly and suddenly, the monopolistic beneficiary of totalitarianism.

One must remember that totalitarianism appeared in the twentieth century as the result of the activities of fanatic and militant teams led by ruthless leaders in combination with resentments nurtured by the lower echelons of the middle class. Presently, in Poland, it is expected that a new middle class will emerge as a beneficial force. And it is expected that the Church may help in consolidating this new middle class, that this class will reject all elements of post-totalitarian decay, and that it will play a decisive role as a herald of rationally oriented processes triggered and monitored by the market economy.

It seems to be clear that the study of totalitarian and post-totalitarian law and its prolonged existence should add important insights to the understanding of these puzzling phenomena. Therefore, it might be useful to extend the examination of these types of law and ask what constitutes the essential feature of the law in general. As a preface to these further considerations, one may hypothesize that if law (in its official and intuitive constructs) embodies power and its underlying conflicts, then it may be regarded as an oppression in frozen form. If this supposition is correct, then power and oppression constitute two faces of the same Janus.

NOTES

1. The term *reification* is usually attributed to George Lukacs. But it was Marcuse who underlined its totalitarian connotations in portraying the technical apparatus of production and distribution as a:

> system which determines *a priori* the product of the apparatus as well as the op-

erations of serving it. In this society, the productive apparatus tends to become totalitarian to the extent to which it determines not only the socially needed occupations, skills and attitudes, but also individual needs and aspirations. . . . Technology serves to institute new, more effective, and more pleasant forms of social control and social cohesion" (Marcuse 1964: xv).

2. It is worthy of note that the government of Jan Olszewski, which had initiated a frontal attack on the post-totalitarian forces and their hidden social structures, was dissolved after only six months in office on June 4, 1992.

6

Law as Petrified Oppression

If quantity could indeed transform itself into quality, an adequate theory of the sociology of law would emerge automatically. The unbelievable number of empirical studies that have been conducted in various countries in the last thirty years (including Ferrari's 1990 contribution of over nine hundred pages) contain ample evidence that the descriptions of the different operations of law in various dispersed areas, cultures, and historical periods have failed, in fact, to generate an empirically grounded theory. The studies have been unable to give even a hint of how one should explain the functioning of law in different social entities.

Paradoxically, when sociological techniques were still at the preintuitive level of development, several impressive (and still valid) synthetic ideas were elaborated, for example, by Durkheim, Weber, or Petrażycki (Górecki 1975). Now, when synthetical theses can draw on an endless accumulation of socioanthropological materials and many interactions, predominantly limited to small-group experiments and explanations, the former are conspicuously absent.

The first task on entering the area of theoretical synthesis is to try to put all the dispersed knowledge into a unifying framework. The Teutonic theory-building approach (based on abstract notions), the Gallic approach (basically the same with some additional elements of wit), and the Nipponic approach based on the seniority structure (Galtung 1981) should be rejected a priori. Since these approaches systematically disregard contact with reality, they tend to find theoretically explanatory results only by chance. What should be more vigorously cultivated is the Anglo-Saxon approach, based on extensive empirical data and supplanted with theoretical elaboration of these data. In short, a methodologically reasonable balance should be struck between diagnosis of the analyzed situation and an appropriate theoretical explanation.

A short but intense look at the history of the development of an empirically oriented sociology of law, and especially its trials and errors, suggests that an attempt to build a comprehensive theory should take the following crucial issues into consideration.

PRELIMINARY THEORETICAL QUESTIONS

1. What is the epistemological status of the descriptive and value-oriented approach in the social sciences? Are descriptions, in fact, hidden values that are manifest in camouflaged form?

2. Is the concept of integrity (not integration) a fruitful starting point for analyzing the possibility of theory building in the sociology of law?

3. Would it be promising to depart from the concept of a monopolistically perceived official law (as a goal-oriented, man-made product) and incorporate intuitive law (the spontaneous product of intersocial relations) into the theory-building process?

4. To what extent should the idea of mutuality ("expectations of expectations," "approved expectations," "justified expectations") be taken as a starting point for analyzing the interpreting empirical data?

5. Can law be understood as a petrified oppression? How is the concept of petrified oppression related to the concept of integrity?

6. Is the hypothesis of a "three-level operation of law" useful for explaining the social operation of law?

7. How is petrified oppression related to power? Is law one of the most manifest forms of power?

8. How do various social systems generate legal systems that are built on the basis of official and intuitive law? How are they connected?

9. Can a legal system be understood as a codified frame of reference based on the elements of an existing social structure?

10. Is the problem of the definition of law (and of the sociology of law) only a semantic issue, or is it also an important point of departure for constituting sociolegal inquiries?

These considerations lead to a conclusion that law should be treated as a petrified oppression. But before this inference is presented in a more elaborate way, several assumptions should be discussed.

PRELIMINARY THEORETICAL ASSUMPTIONS

The Nature of Value Judgements

The question of whether values are the by-products of the cognitive-rational structure of the human mind or whether descriptions are the by-products of the value-oriented attitudes of humans is still an open one.

In traditional theories of law or jurisprudence, the idea that *Sein* and *Sollen* ("is" and "should be") represent two completely different, separate worlds is accepted as dogma. Indeed, all attempts to reduce "should be" to "is" remain unsuccessful. In other words, one cannot logically deduce from the existing state of affairs what should be (what should take place) in the normative area. These two spheres of existential reality, according to the currently accepted methodological point of view, have to be totally separated epistemologically.

According to this paradigm, the elements of normative command elude all attempts at descriptive analysis and are treated as being beyond the reach of any factual assessments. As a result, speculation arises about this mysterious, value-laden ingredient. Some theoreticians endow it with a natural genesis; some ascribe to it a religious source; others look for its semantic or logical grounds. It might be interesting to try to find why speculation goes mainly from "is" to "should be."

But why not reverse the problem and ask to what extent "is" could be explained by its reduction to "should be"? It seems plausible to assume that descriptive reality is nothing else but the by-product of the disintegration of normative reality; in other words, that normative reality in its functioning generates various side effect elements of cognitive understanding. If this is accepted, then the reality of "should be" appears, paradoxically, as the primordial, essential, basic type of reality, whereas the seemingly elementary reality of description appears as a by-product of the comprehension and operation of normative reality. This point of comprehension assumes that the primordial normative reality is based on the teleological paradigm, which prescribes *what should be done in order to achieve what is desired.*

It is useful to recall that human beings, in their individual and collective (and sequential in developing common "collective representations") history, do not appear as reflective existences, but manifest themselves as active agents. To achieve something one has to be equipped with the proper scheme (or schemata) for acting. Acting is primary. It manifests itself in all practical undertakings. The thinking process is mainly the storing and polishing of those paradigms of efficient action (individual and social) that have proven gainful in human life. It may thus be assumed that each new teleological (aim-directed) paradigm that is recorded as useful (or not useful) on the market of human experience is consequently broken down into simpler elements, which, in turn, are expressed in a descriptive manner. Thus, they are nothing else but elements that have been cognitively elaborated, preserved, classified, and put into systematic order—hidden and transformed normative elements. In the midst of this "purifying" process, they are shorn off from their origin and start to live as seemingly autonomous cognitive particles. Further, they then appear as being so remote from their epistemological grounds that they assume a new epistemological character.

If these assumptions are correct, then all norms (as imperative recommendations that are oriented toward "should be") are, more or less, functional. Thus the norm "do not kill" is a shortcut of the norm "if you kill, you destroy the peaceful life of the community, and in the interests of social order, you will be subjected to the oppressive force of social control"; the norm "pay back your obligations" is a shortcut of the norm "if you do not pay your obligations, you spoil the harmonious circulation of goods and services, and place yourself as a social outcast—and in effect, nobody will cooperate with you"; and the norm "obey your legitimized authority" is a shortcut of the norm "if you are not obedient to the legitimized authorities, you destroy the chain of command, so the entrusted agents will use their accumulated might to oppress you." Generally speaking, each norm has its own functional, currently invisible, hidden nosological roots. Speaking more generally, each value is a shortcut of a goal-oriented, aim-targeted statement. Instead of announcing that something is "gainful" or "punishing" from the point of view of its consequences for an individual or a social group, the manifested value simply states "good" or "bad."

Thus, the first mystery to be tackled in the quest for an empirically grounded theory of the sociology of law is the nature of value judgements. The second mystery is connected with the notion of oppression, which will be discussed later.

Social Integrity

In sociological literature, the problem of the integrative function of law has been discussed from many different angles. For Durkheim, it was mainly a "solidarity" type of integration that tended to secure social cohesion on the basis of common attitudes and cooperation. The main goal of this integrative function was to incorporate morality into the framework of social life. Petrażycki's integrative understanding was connected to the organizational function of the law (the construction of institutions and organizations). It is well known that the Parsonian integrative function was construed as uniting subsystems within a general social system that was known as "AGIL": "A," adaptation; "G," goal-attainment; "I," integration; and "L," latency. Habermas's complicated ideas on integration could be simplified as the understanding of the integration of actions through rationalizations on two levels: life-world, and the larger scale social system and its subsystems.

Here, social integrity is understood in a neutral way. It may operate differently than in Durkheim's understanding for negative goals like regulations in the extermination camps; it may apply the integrity axis to irrational social movements differently from Habermas's understanding; or it may cement a subsystem such as the Mafia to the general social system. As dignity is a manifestation of integrity in an individual (a criminal can have his own type of "dignity" as well—consider for example, the "real man" in Sykes 1974: 104), so law furnishes a given social system with the integrity it needs for survival. Law is a neutral type of integrity, a "backbone" of the social system, a straitjacket that supplies this system with its internal cohesion.

It is not only *official law* that keeps social systems together and provides them with integrity; they are supported by intuitive law as well. The official law is written law (law in the books) executed by state officials. *Intuitive law* is a mutually accepted relationship of claims and duties. Although certain elements of official law may enter into the picture (a judge who decides not according to the letter of the law but in accordance with his/her individual understanding of the situation, or a private mediator who uses written law to solve a conflict brought to him by the joint agreement of those concerned), a single element of intuitive law is sufficient to make it operative. Official law is constructed by the state (acknowledged officials) and its agencies (norms enacted according to established procedure); intuitive law relies on a set of mutually agreed-upon norms sanctioned by the internal acceptance of the concerned parties.

Perhaps it is not important that the concept of intuitive law (Erlich's "living law") was first introduced by Petrażycki (Podgórecki 1991: 11). It is also not important to label it as unwritten law, social law, folk law, natural law, informal law, and so on. It is significant that the official law—studied in law schools, used by government clerks, applied by prosecutors, judges, and the police—is understood as the only legitimate type of law. Thus, the law upheld by the indigenous or "visible" minorities in Canada, the United States, Australia, New Zealand, Holland (Moluccans and Surinam people) and other countries is deprived by the officials in charge of the dignity of law. Only officials have the right to decide what does and does not belong in the category of law. Likewise, indigenous people or other minorities perceive their own law as the only valid law and believe that the laws of the countries they live in have been imposed on them by strangers whose way of life runs contrary to the canons of nature, in short, that it is invalid law. Contemporary theories of law only gradually, and under various terms like "pluralistic legal systems" and "private law," begin to recognize the existence and social or political relevance of intuitive law.

Official and intuitive laws are complementary. Under the oppressive regime of totalitarian law—whose formal appearance is sometimes quite elegant (and eloquent) and full of empty respect for human rights, but whose execution is arbitrary and cruel—intuitive law enters into the picture. It tends to operate at the level of basic human needs: it develops the whole underworld structure of the "second economy" (Łoś 1990). This economy, illegal from the point of view of official law, allows recourse to available help, without which populations might starve or perish. In its task of developing the "underworld" of a second economy, intuitive law is eu-functional (advantageous) for the given social entity. From one point of view, it satisfies the needs of the population, but from another, it supports the official establishment.

Mutuality

The concept of intuitive law shows quite clearly that the mutual agreement that helps to maintain certain types of equilibrium among interested parties is essential. Again, it is less important to determine who first fully formulated this idea.[1]

What is important is that the reciprocity established by mutually binding claims and duties is a useful element for building a theory of the sociology of law. Thus, in the area of legal behavior and legal attitudes, one may also speak about "justified expectations" when expectations are approved in advance by the second party. One may speak about "approved expectations," which are sanctioned by the opposite side.

In comparison, the theory of the sociology of morality would need an assumption of a lack of mutuality; an assumption of the existence of a unidirectional type of link, a sole-duty type of relationship. Indeed, an empirical investigation of moral phenomena should reveal that people would not accept a demand directed toward them in a case where they felt morally obliged to do something. They would say, "I feel that it is my duty to behave in this way, but no one among those who are the potential 'targets' of my duty has a legitimate right to demand that I behave in this way."

It is important to notice that integrity plays the same role for official law as for intuitive law. In both cases, the requirement of integrity puts together diverse elements in a coherent scheme of reciprocity.

Law as Petrified Oppression

What does it mean to say that law can be understood as a petrified oppression? Since duties are the essential ingredients of law, and since they restrict human behavior, then to the extent that restrictions of human behavior constitute oppression, the law oppresses human behavior. The elusive phenomenon of power should be comprehended as the relation between duties and rights as manifested in certain spheres of human behavior. Consequently, the more duties, the more oppression, and the more rights, the less oppression. The heavier the oppression, the stronger the power, and the weaker the power, the milder the oppression.

Law is oppressive in a triple sense. First, it is oppressive per se, since it limits the available options of human activity, quite often physically compelling certain types of repulsive behavior. Second, it persecutes certain behaviors and employs the whole machinery of social control (primary, secondary, or tertiary) in case of trespass against its own rules, threatening to use this machinery in advance. Third, it plays a basic role in distributing various kinds of pressure (taxes, charges, penalties, duties, tariffs, burdens, etc.).

One of the most characteristic features of law is the sanctions attached to it. These sanctions can be formal, as in the case of official law, or informal, as in the area of intuitive law. The Polish workers' courts referred to in Chapter 2 attached new types of condemnation to the usual formal sanctions. "Peer opinion" was used against the Looking-glass selves of those who had been the targets in this justice regime (Podgórecki 1974: 150–61). In short, justice based on the concept of "losing face" was supposed to supplement justice based on the concept of guilt; in other words, formal sanctions were strengthened by informal ones. The use of informal sanctions, or a publicly announced warning that they might be used, was introduced to anchor or petrify oppression by forbidding certain types of behavior.

In this sense, the law itself constitutes a petrified oppression. By using formal or informal (in the case of intuitive law) sanctions, it channels behavior in the direction that is desired by the current lawmaker. It might be useful to mention that formal sanctions, although they are regarded by classical jurisprudence as primary legal factors, have only secondary importance. They enter into the social picture only when the prestige of the law is not strong enough to secure the needed support. Those who do not understand the nature of the clash between official and native law underestimate, as a rule, the importance of the prestige of law based on traditional or communally sanctioned grounds.

SUBSTANTIVE THEORETICAL THESES

Three-Level Operation of Law

The hypothesis of the "three-level operation of the law" is a useful middle-range thesis for describing the functioning of law in various social settings (Podgórecki 1974; 1991: 9–37). This thesis suggests that the law operates on three different levels: the level of the social system, the level of various subcultures, and the level of the acting individual's psyche. If a prolegal psyche has support from a prolegal subculture, and if both factors operate in a generally conformist societal framework, then support for a given social norm is optimal. If the antilegal attitudes of an individual find encouragement in a negativist legal subculture, and if both these factors operate inside a rebellious society, then support for the given social norm is minimal.

At the level of the individual psyche, there are several distinct legal-personality structures. These are: (1) the posture of Kantian legalism (the categoric imperative to follow the law); (2) prolegal and internally supportive feedback mechanisms; (3) legal kamikaze; (4) legal warpedness (the existence of a destructive antilegal "virus"); (5) double legal reinforcement; (6) the position of a subversive antilegalist; and (7) "dirty togetherness" (Podgórecki 1983: 33).

Of course, these individual factors, as well as the subcultural and societal factors, have various weights and may appear in different constellations. All these elements may change the operation of the law considerably; they may also alter its effectiveness. Nevertheless, this hypothesis provides a general framework for a description and explanation of the operation of the law in society in general. If a diagnosis of various factors as they exist in a given society is accomplished, this hypothesis may furnish a description and an explanation of the function of law in that particular society.

Law and Power

The law may be understood as a petrified oppression. What does this mean? Oppression has already been defined as the man-made limitation of available options of human behavior. This understanding takes into consideration the fact that human behavior may play itself out in various directions and that there exist certain obstructive, internal or external, restrictions on this behavior. Certain legal restrictions, like certain physical barriers, alter human behavior. Thus, law, in general, may be understood as the sum of all specific normative restrictions, a metatype restriction. The law freezes existing options of human behaviors, allowing them to appear only in certain areas and in certain forms. Official rights are restricted from outside by reference to the binding legal system. Although intuitive rights are accepted only from inside, they operate as legitimized by the concerned parties as a result of an informal process of law-creating negotiation. In this sense, the intuitive law is also externally binding. Therefore, legal rights and obligations cannot be modified by the wish of an individually acting agent.

The law, then, imposes various types of restrictions and, at the same time, transforms itself into—and becomes petrified as—oppression. From an internal point of view, this process may appear as self-discipline; from an external point of view, it imposes oppression. Garland clearly summarizes Foucault's view:

> According to Foucault, it was ultimately the generalization of discipline which underpinned and made possible the generalization of democratic constitutions and the expansions of liberal forms of freedom. Without this vast infrastructure of power relations which subjected the masses to an orderly, disciplined existence, the extension of "liberty" could never have taken place. This echoes the Hobbesian argument that freedom under the law implies a prior process of subjugation, and it constitutes the meaning of Foucault's suggestion that discipline is "the dark side" of democracy and its egalitarian laws. . . . The disciplines ensure that real constraints and controls are introduced into relationships which law deems to be voluntary or contractual, thus permitting the coexistence of legal freedom and habitual domination. It is in this sense that the disciplines are said to be "a sort of a counter-law" (Garland 1990: 147).

How is the concept of law (petrified oppression) related to integrity? As noted previously, self-discipline may lead to the establishment of internal integrity. Apparently, law (as an external factor) may contribute as well to the development of integrity. Hobbes's view of human nature is usually considered to be pessimistic. He believed that those with similar abilities who aspire to the same things must as a matter of course become enemies and distrust one another. This competition and distrust leads to a state of continuous "war of all against all." Thus, people live in a state of "continual fear, and danger of violent death; And the life of man, solitary, poor, nasty, brutish, and short" (Hobbes 1968 [1651]: 186).

More than a century before Hobbes, Machiavelli (1988: 59) expressed a similar idea about human nature:

> For this may be said of men generally: they are ungrateful, fickle, feigners and dissemblers, avoiders of danger, eager to gain. While you benefit them they are devoted to you; they would shed their blood for you; they would offer their possessions, their lives, and their sons, as I said before, when the need to do so is far off. But when you are hard pressed, they turn away.

In the modern world, largely because of the "rationalization processes" that keep various types of oppression under steady control, human nature can be best observed in special microworlds, especially in situations where accumulated oppression removes various social selves and masks and leaves human beings "naked." These microcosms are especially transparent in prisons. The classical study by Sykes gives a good account of the dense accretion of pain brought about by deprivation of liberty, goods, services, heterosexual relationships, autonomy, and security. The harder these deprivations, the greater the frustrations of the inmates and the greater the clash of their various roles (Sykes 1974).

A Polish study on the inmates of correctional institutions presents additional data and elaborates on some of the hypotheses that elucidate this situation. According to this study, the frustration of the inmates could be directed only in part toward the authorities. The strength of the authorities was too overwhelming and the pool of possible punishments too broad for the inmates to start a war with those in command. Therefore, it seemed more useful to direct their accumulated frustration against their peers. But since such a situation could also lead to an uncontrolled "war of all against all," it was more rational, in the Weberian sense, to find an instrumental solution stratifying the community of inmates into several categories. Thus, the inmates were divided roughly into two strata: (1) "men" (lords) who have full power; and (2) "suckers" (slaves) who have no rights. This stratification was fully protected from the eyes of the teachers and guardians, which gave the community of inmates a sense of independence and intimacy. The evident function of this stratification was to ensure that the "men" had a means of elevating themselves above the humiliating and degrading situation of captivity. The possibility of exploiting a "sucker" (including sexual exploitation), or the arbitrary punishment of a sucker could give a man a feeling of superiority (Podgórecki and Łoś 1979: 23–24). This artificial stratification, it was hypothesized, might confine the potential "war of all against all" to a manageable size and provide at least some inmates with "dignity," albeit artificial. This stratified type of oppression was sanctioned, in this particular case, by the provisions of the iron rule of intuitive law.

Social Systems

How do various social systems generate corresponding legal systems? How are they affected by the functioning of the legal systems?

Coleman was very perceptive:

An especially unfortunate consequence of the loss of a theory of action was loss of contact with that one discipline that arguably should have the strongest intellectual links to social theory: common and constitutional law. One might even argue that law, as a set of rules having a high degree of internal consistency, as well as principles behind these rules, has as strong a claim to constitute social theory as does any alternative body of principles offered up by sociologists. All case law is based inherently on a theory of action (Coleman 1986).

A study devoted to the problematic relations between social and legal systems that regarded as its main goal an orderly collection of data could provide a starting point for future theoretical investigation in this area (Podgórecki, Whelan, and Khosla 1985).

Some attempts to formulate generalizations of this type can be found in a neglected study of Lidz (1979). Perhaps this unfortunate neglect is due to his having overemphasized the normative, value-laden concept of "solidarity." However, Lidz has formulated four basic types of linkage between social and legal systems:

1. When specifically societal solidarity is highly evolved, as in the nations of the modern West, the law and formal legality will be highly developed;

2. Where solidarity devolves mainly upon primordial groups and diffuses social ties, as in classical China, the normative order will stress less formal kinds of social control;

3. Where the formal aspects of ties of societal solidarity are widely sacrificed to expediency, the procedural integrity of the law may be routinely undermined as in Nazi Germany and other "fascist" nations;

4. Where stress on social change and collective mobilization overrides the stability of communal solidarity among members of society, as in Soviet Russia, the "command society" cannot accept the systematic constraints of law in a thoroughgoing way (Weber, Fuller, Solzhenitsyn, and Berman in Lidz 1979: 23–24).

In Lidz's understanding, the meaning of "solidarity" is apparently determined by values coming from the current ruling elite.

Probably the most advanced formal model of the interplay between the social and legal systems was presented by Evan (1990: 222–23). Here are four examples of the more specific relationships which constitute the thirty elements of this model:

1. The level of societal inequality (8) is positively related to the level of societal conflict (9) . . . 6. The rate of change of legal system VNRO (13) is associated with the level of societal inequality. . . . 9. The level of legitimacy of legal system (16) is positively related to the rate of compliance of the citizenry of law (17) . . . 11. The level of societal conflicts (18, 19, 26, 27) is negatively related to the level of legitimacy of the non-legal subsystems of a society (20, 21, 28, 29) (Evan 1990: 228).

Although the theoretical attempts presented above are methodologically attractive, one may nonetheless accept Coleman's suggestion that the agglomerated potential of legal sciences serves as another good starting point. Hence it might also be useful to consider the better-recognized types or families of legal systems. Reflections on the so-called families of law single out several categories of legal systems (Krislow 1985: 25–38) from which the following typology is derived: (1) legal systems based on codes (Romanistic-German); (2) common-law legal systems; (3) totalitarian legal systems; and (4) legal systems based on nonlegal premises. Again, following the discussion on legal families (summarized by Krislow), it might be useful to employ two criteria: (1) the type of legal concepts; and (2) the style of legal thinking.

Legal System Codified

The family of legal systems based on codes (Romanistic-German) is characterized by a distinct set of legal principles, the clarity of legal notions, and especially by the consistent legal statutes that consolidate various legal notions into a united body of binding law. Not only do these codes tend to synthesize the existing socioeconomic experience generated by the given social system; they also tend to cover all real and social possibilities with a preconceived set of cognitive ideas. In addition, these codes tend to influence socioeconomic reality by channelling human behavior according to certain beliefs pertaining to the social systems in which they operate. The legal codes that belong to the family of Roman-German legal systems have a tendency to develop a distinctive school of legal thinking that flows from top to bottom. This school of legal thinking is thought to be characterized by the logical thinking in the interpretation of legal concepts, which is also characteristic of legislative lawmaking (Aubert 1983: 77–97).

Common-law legal systems are entirely different. They are based on grass-roots wisdom, which is conceived on the empirical level of human interactions and flows from bottom to top. These systems are a priori reluctant to accept any preconceived legal notions that are not tested by day-to-day experiences. These systems incorporate and assimilate into their own stockpile of legal wisdoms only those legal concepts that have been generated by the actual needs and clashes of legal subjects cooperating or competing among themselves. Their logic is instrumental, invented ad hoc, skeptical toward large schemes and ironclad canons of deduction. In principle, these legal systems are reacting to, or coming from, outside social stimuli. The elements of these systems grow in steady response to the constant flow of questions formulated by the conflicts of human tasks and interests. They subsume a considerable amount of inertia. This may be socially beneficial since it precludes an easy departure from the well-established social patterns of coexistence, but it might also be socially harmful since it may not leave enough room for innovations that promote social changes.

Both legal systems based on codes and common-law legal systems are generated in societies that have developed a rather high of democratic spirit. Both types may be regarded as responses to a societal need to address and possibly reshape the economic and sociopolitical problems of their time. They are basically open systems. They contain mechanisms for social change that enable them to adapt existing legal arrangements to the pressures of social expectations. In the case of legal systems based on codes, parliaments assume the guiding function. In legal systems based on common law, the maieutic function is assumed by an elaborated system of courts (this is why the beginnings of the American sociology of law understood the empirical definitions of law as rules that had been established by the courts). In general, democratic legal systems redirect social oppression in a way that is "tolerated" by the main forces of the existing social structure. Social relationships are supported by contractual arrangements or by mutually agreed upon intuitive rules. Mutuality appears to be the guiding principal that regulates relations among members of democratic legal systems based on legal codes and a system of common-law systems.

There exist also legal systems that are based on codes of a closed character. These systems have a directly oppressive character. They are totalitarian legal systems. It was shown earlier that their legal codes contain the will of the ruling party and embody in this will the essence of the ideology elaborated by the party. These systems are closed (contrary to the proclamations contained in their constitutions that aim at creating a desirable propaganda image); they are open only to the changeable currents in the ideology of the ruling party. These systems are characterized by an inherent schizophrenia: they pronounce something legally attractive (mainly for international consumption), but they practice its opposite. To some, they may appear as democratic since only the silenced insiders are familiar with the everyday practice of these systems. They are regarded as instruments of social engineering, but social engineering of a "dark" character (Podgórecki 1990: 66–67). Thus, the social lie is an inherent ingredient of such systems.

Although the legal profession eagerly plays its role in clarifying the basic concepts of totalitarian legal systems and develops parallel styles of legal reasoning, the practice that accompanies the applications of these systems is especially revealing. The primary goal of such legal systems is to serve as an instrument for pressuring people into behaving contrary to their wishes. Thus, totalitarian legal systems are openly repressive; they not only redistribute oppression within the society but they oppress the society as a whole. These systems are built on the official law through which they develop a complicated system (and sometimes an additional metasystem or metasystems) of social control. Intuitive law, although it exists on the system's periphery, and although it is usually treated as an illegal social pathology, tries to make up for instances of striking injustice. The rule of mutuality appears mainly on the level of intuitive law. This rule, with some exceptions in civil law, is alien to the official structure of the law.

Entirely different legal systems based on the concept of the "decent man," or on religious premises, represent the last category of legal systems. In this case, the social system develops a model of approved behavior, sometimes adding to this model ritualistic manners of action, sometimes linking it directly to religious liturgy, prescribing in this way an expected style of behavior. In this type of system, the law plays only a secondary role, simply providing a way of linking the citizenry to the authorities or of prescribing the obligatory relationship between citizen and ruler. Internal, community-oriented activities remain under the rule of the model of the "decent man." In these tight, small circles, everything is socially transparent, and members of the community judge others and are judged on the basis of their life performances. In consequence, official law is reserved for dealing with the matters of the state. Thus, in systems based on the concept of the decent man, official law plays, as a rule, a directly oppressive role; it supports and defends the interests of the ruler (or the ruling elite). This law rejects the rule of reciprocity on principle. It dictates to its subjects what duties they must fulfill in order to please the ruler. Intuitive law flourishes in small communal circles; only there is this type of law structured according to the rule of reciprocity. There, reciprocity may deal with services and goods or may offer various types of protection for certain benefits.

Defining Law

Is the problem of defining a sociology of law only a semantic issue or does it have more profound theoretical repercussions?

Some scholars maintain that the sociology of law deals mainly with empty issues: "I sense that our field is running so smoothly along familiar tracks that the questions and answers have begun to sound a comfortable, but rather boring, "clackety-clack" (quoted after Macaulay 1984: 150). Certain other scholars discard the problem of defining the sociology of law as irrelevant. It is difficult to judge whether they are so frustrated by cognitive difficulties, or blinded or even fascinated by the very possibility of conducting research in previously inaccessible sociolegal areas, that they think it is a premature undertaking, or whether they are simply unable to present any new synthetic generalizations or adequate definitions. Probably the most interesting attempts to formulate such definitions are listed by Evan (1990: 19–23).

Nonetheless, previous deliberations suggest the following definition: *the sociology of law deals with relationships among various factors that are treated as independent or dependent variables operating on various levels of society, while petrified oppression and the integrity of social systems are regarded as essential factors of these operations.*

This definition indicates, on a descriptive level, the area of inquiry particular to the sociology of law, and also indicates that the sociology of law is an empirical social science that tries to refute or prove social regularities. On a theoretical level, it indicates indirectly that the central problem for the sociology of law is the relationship between corresponding social and legal systems, and points, finally, to social oppression and social integrity as crucial factors that link together the social and legal systems.

SUMMARY

In Plato's *Republic*, Thrasymachus maintained that law and morality had been invented by the strong to subjugate and manipulate the weak. Callicles, his opponent, contended that law and morality were invented by the weak as a defense against the strong. In totalitarian systems, the strong indeed use official law to control the weak, but the weak use intuitive law to defend themselves against the strong. In democratic societies (particularly welfare states), those who are economically weak are sometimes politically strong and use the law to defend themselves against the economically strong. In sociolegal systems dominated by the concept of the "decent man," two parallel normative realities seem to coexist. Thus, under the dominion of official law, a subject does not have a chance to escape the overpowering regime of the ruler, and the dominion of intuitive law is difficult for the official ruler to penetrate.

What Durkheim said implicitly was later explicitly developed by Erikson (1966). The main thesis of Erikson's book states that certain rates and types of spontaneous or socially construed "social pathology" are needed to maintain a certain level and type of social control, and that this level and type of social control is required to ensure the social integrity of the given social system. This resembles a vicious circle: integrity is the inherent feature of law, the law maintains social order and suppresses deviance, but deviance itself is needed to invoke and maintain integrity.

It would be a mistake to assume that only official law may perform oppressive functions. Intuitive law may play an oppressive role as well. As already indicated, intuitive law is mobilized to create a quasi-family in order to surround one of its members emotionally and economically, as happens in the underworld of prostitution (see Chapter 1); when the title "wife-in-law" is bestowed, the law is performing a tyrannical task

(Romenesko and Miller 1989). In this example, traditional family relations are used as a modern form of the pimp-prostitute relationship for male economic exploitation of women; intuitive law is used to preserve the integrity of a patriarchal world structured by men.

The law is oppressive in a triple sense. First, it is oppressive per se, since it limits available options of human activity. Sometimes this oppression is very light, as with indicating when to cross the street. As a rule, however, the law compels human beings to perform in ways that are anathema to them. Totalitarian law provides an extreme example of such compulsion. Second, the law persecutes certain behaviors by prohibiting them and employs the whole machinery of sanctions against the trespass of rules regarded as binding; it also threatens its subjects in advance with the application of its compulsive apparatus of social control (particularly in the realm of criminal law). Third, the law (especially civil law) plays the decisive role in allocating various forms of pressure (taxes, charges, payments, penalties, duties, tariffs, burdens, reimbursements, etc.).

Each type of legal system contains a different type of accumulated social wisdom. Code-structured legal systems tend to provide their social systems with rationally structured guidance. Common-law legal systems furnish the social systems in which they operate with a variety of monitoring-adjustment-feedback mechanisms. Totalitarian legal systems, using ideology and force, effectively press their social systems to perform those tasks that are repulsive to the majority of their members. The hidden wisdom of legal systems based on the concept of the "decent man" is to disregard the official law as the main instrument of social interaction and to maintain the integrity of the system through the use of intuitive law.

According to one perception, social oppression is the result of the clash between various types of interests and those who intend to execute these interests. However, some forms of social oppression may remain in a "dormant" state as long as the activities of certain political parties, the intelligentsia in Eastern Europe, students, "Greens," feminists, aboriginal people, and so on do not bring them to life. Should this happen, their oppressive character becomes suddenly visible.

Thus, the sociology of law deals with the relationships between various social factors (including legal factors), which are either treated as independent factors (code-structured legal systems and especially totalitarian legal systems), or as dependent factors (common-law systems) operating on different levels of societal interactions. Law as a petrified oppression, then, always keeps the integrity of the social system intact.

NOTE

1. Was it Petrażycki when he spoke, in his hermetic language, about the interrelations between passively/actively structured impulsions? Was it Mali-

nowski who, using his anthropological experience, pointed to the mutuality of the exchange of goods and services? Was it Gouldner who, in his attempt to trace the roots of the concept of reciprocity to the Greek past, elevated the idea of reciprocity to the basic type of human relationship? Was it the theoretical school of sociology, called *exchange theory* (Skinner, Goode, Homans, Levi-Strauss, and others), that gave additional data and arguments to support the thesis that law is based on mutuality? Is it Luhmann who, in his unnecessarily complicated Teutonic manner, brings once more to scholarly attention this already well-elaborated concept?

7

Conclusions

The main task of this volume has been to specify those basic features of social oppression that distinguish it from the other social phenomena. Various studies taken mainly from social psychology have been employed to enlighten and explain this widespread element of human life that has nonetheless been overlooked.

From the beginning, it became clear that the phenomenon of "I," theoretically neglected until recently, should play one of the central roles in these deliberations. Different types of selves appeared important not only because they are the essential components of the individual atomlike psyche but also because they play the unrecognized role of implanted societal agents, which may oppress individuals from inside. The selves are formed by the expectations of socialization processes to ensure this outcome, which is supposed to be tested through the continuous process of trial and error, as beneficial for the society as a whole. Therefore, social control has two important dimensions: the external—as an organized apparatus imposing on the community the imperative of conformity—and the internal—as a cluster of invisible elements designed to play similar roles, but performed from inside.

In the past and present literature, many impressive descriptions of psychological factors playing roles of oppressive tormenters can be found. For example, "The basis of shame is not some personal mistake of ours, but the ignominy, the humiliation we feel that we must be what we are without any choice in the matter, and that this humiliation is seen by everyone" (Kundera 1992: 248). But for the current study, relevant were these illustrations that shed some light on the modern type of oppression.

The overview of the most significant studies concerning social oppression revealed that, under the regime of oppression, conformism does not manifest itself as the dominant type of behavior in everyday life. Under oppression, withdrawal and hyperconformism emerge as the most significant categories of behavior. Also, adaptation shifts its main strategies from its primary forms of adjustment (those that tailor means to be in harmony with conventional aims) to the patterns of secondary adjustment (those patterns that tend to employ illegal means). These considerations, and especially those that dealt with the phenomenon of obedience, pointed out that norms of a legal character, whether official (approved by the state) or intuitive (accepted by the parties involved), are the primary instruments applied in regulating social order.

Law in the multitude of its deviations has been investigated, since illegal means play an important role under the regime of oppression. As the basic conclusion of these inquiries, an idea emerged that in a totalitarian setting (and this constitutes the core of its pathological version), the law has only a *conditional* validity. This validity depends on hidden political forces that use various legal structures in a seemingly whimsical—but, in fact, well-calculated—manner.

It was further assumed that during the prolonged period of the regime of pathological governance, the law not only openly abuses traditional legal principles but also violates the moral and intuitive attitudes of the populace. This pathological regime injects into these attitudes "psychic venoms" that, by inertia, have a tendency to act in circumstances when the dominant totalitarian framework has already been destroyed. These assumptions were tested against the historical reality of one particular society—Polish society.

Using the above conjectures, a new understanding of the law emerges: that it is not so much *external* sanctions as assumed by classical jurisprudence (although, from the official-law perspective, external sanctions are crucial), but the *internal* elements of the socially constructed selves, manifested by intuitive law, that are decisive for the operations of the law. In consequence, the law must be seen as a petrified, double— sometimes mainly external and sometimes mainly internal—oppression.

The final conclusion is that (1) social oppression may in some instances have an exclusively regulatory nature, usually punishing and regressive in its essence, and (2) social oppression can be introduced into social life not only by direct commands of explicit legal norms but may also ensue from a general legal culture.

Bibliography

Adelson, A., and R. Lapides. *Lodz Ghetto*. New York: Viking, 1989.

Adorno, T., L. Frenkel-Brunswick, D. Levinson, and R. Sanford. *The Authoritarian Personality*. New York: Harper and Row, 1950.

Arenas, R. *Old Rosa*. New York: Grove Press, 1989.

Arendt, H. *The Origins of Totalitarianism*. London: George Allen & Unwin, 1962.

Atkinson, R., and G. Lee. "Brutality in Soviet Army has Ethnic Overtones." *Manchester Guardian Weekly* 143: 23, 1990.

Aubert, V. *The Hidden Society*. Totowa, N.J.: Bedminster Press, 1965.

————. *In Search of Law*. Oxford: Martin Robertson, 1983.

Barnett, H. G. "The Nature of Potlatch." *American Anthropology* 40, 1938.

Bendix, R. *Max Weber—An Intellectual Portrait*. Berkeley: University of California Press, 1977.

Berelson, B., and G. Steiner. *Human Behavior*. New York: Harcourt Brace and World, 1964.

Bettelheim, B., "Individual and Mass Behaviour in Extreme Situations," *Journal of Abnormal and Social Psychology* 38 (4): 417–52, Oct. 1943.

Blackburn, Robin. "Defining Slavery—Its Special Feature and Special Role." In *Slavery and Other Forms of Unfree Labour*, edited by Leonie Archer. London: Routledge & Kegan Paul, 1988.

Brzezinski, Z. *The Grand Failure*. New York, Charles Scribner's Sons, 1989.

Bukowski, V. *To Build a Castle*. London: Andre Deutsch, 1978.

Camus, A. *The Plague*. Middlesex: Penguin Books, 1977.

Cheng, Nien. *Life and Death in Shanghai*. New York: Grove Press, 1986.

Chodorow, N. *The Reproduction of Mothering*. Berkeley: University of California Press, 1978.

Christie, R., and F. L. Geis. *Studies in Machiavellianism*. New York: Academic Press, 1970.

Codere, H. *Fighting with Property*. Seattle: University of Washington Press, 1950.

Coleman, J. "Social Theorem, Social Research, and Theory of Action." *American Journal of Sociology* 1309, 1986.

Cooley, C. *Human Nature and Social Order*. New Jersey: Scribner's, 1902.

Crossman, R., ed. *The God That Failed*. London: Hamish Hamilton, 1950.

Creative Choices. The Report of the Task Force on Federally Sentenced Women. Ottawa, Correctional Services, 1990.

Curry, J., and J. Wasilewski. "Nomenclatura o sobie" (Nomenclature about itself). *Polityka* 37, September 1989.

Dawidowicz, L. S. *The War Against the Jews 1933–1945*. New York: Seth Press, 1975.

de Beauvoir, S. *The Woman Destroyed*. London: Flamingo, 1988.

Del Boca, A., and M. Giovana. *Fascism Today*. London: Heinemann, 1970.

Des Pres, T. *The Survivor*. New York: Oxford University Press, 1980.

Ellul, J. *Propaganda*. New York: Vintage, 1967.

Elster, J., ed. *The Multiple Self*. Cambridge: Cambridge University Press, 1985.

Erikson, K. *Wayward Puritans*. New York: John Wiley, 1966.

Evan, W. *Social Structure and Law*. Newbury Park, CA: Sage, 1990.

Ferrari, V., ed. *Developing Sociology of Law*. Milan: Giuffre, 1990.

Foucault, M. *Power-Knowledge*. New York: Pantheon Books, 1980.

Fredro-Boniecki, T. *Zwyciestwo Ksiedza Jerzego* (*The Victory of Father Jerzy*). Warsaw: Niezalezna Spolka Wydawnicza, 1990.

Freund, J. *The Sociology of Max Weber*. Penguin, 1972.

Friedrich, C., ed. *Totalitarianism*. Cambridge: Harvard University Press, 1954.

Friedrich, C., and Z. Brzezinski. *Totalitarian Dictatorship and Autocracy*. Cambridge: Harvard University Press, 1965.

Fromm, E. *The Fear of Freedom*. London: Routledge & Kegan Paul, 1942.

Galtung, J. "Structure, Culture and Intellectual Style." *Social Science Information* 20, 1981.

Garfinkel, H. "Conditions of Successful Degradation Ceremonies." *American Journal of Sociology* 61: 5, 1965.

Garland, D. *Punishment and Modern Society*. Chicago: University of Chicago Press, 1990.

Gella, A. *Development of Class Structure in Eastern Europe*. Albany: State University of New York Press, 1989.

Gephart, W. "The Totalitarian Use of Symbols in the Nazis' Perversion of the Law." Paper presented during the Sociological Conference in Madrid, July 1990.

Gerbing, D., and W. Buskist. *Psychology Boundaries and Frontiers*. Glenview, IL: HarperCollins, 1990.

Giddens, A. *New Rules of Sociological Method*. London: Hutchinson, 1976.

Glasser, R. J. *365 Days*. New York: George Braziller, 1971.

Goffman, I. *Asylums*. New York: Anchor Books, 1961.

Goldberg, I. *Oppression and Social Intervention*. Chicago: Nelson-Hall, 1978.

Goldfarb, J. C. *Beyond Glasnost: The Post-Totalitarian Mind*. Chicago: University of Chicago Press, 1989.

Górecki, J., ed. *Sociology and Jurisprudence of Leon Petrazycki*. Urbana: University of Illinois Press, 1975.

Grygier, T. *Oppression: A Study in Social and Criminal Psychology*. London: Routledge & Kegan Paul, 1943; New York: Grove Press, 1973.

Grześkowiak, A. "Tajne Sady w PRL" (Secret Courts in PRL). *Tygodnik Powszechny*, NR. 28/29, 1989.

Halberstam, D. *Making of a Quagmire*. New York: Random House, 1965.

Hansson, D. "The Patchwork Quilt of Power Relations: A Challenge to South African Feminism." Paper presented during The International Feminist Conference on Women, Law and Social Control, Montreal, Canada, 1991.

Hartsock, N. C. "The Feminist Standpoint." In *Feminism and Methodology*, edited by S. Harding. Bloomington: Indiana University Press, 1987.

Hobbes, T. *Leviathan*. [1651]. Harmondsworth, England: Penguin, 1968.

Ignatieff, M. *A Just Measure of Pain*. New York: Pantheon Books, 1978.

Kitzinger, S. *Women as Mothers*. Glasgow: Fontana/Collins, 1978.

Havel, V. *Summer Meditations*. Toronto: Alfred A. Knopf, Canada, 1992.

Koestler, A. In R. Crossman, ed. *The God that Failed*. London: Hamish Hamilton, 1950.

Kojder, A., ed. *Przymus w Spoleczenstwie (Oppression in Society)*. Warsaw: Polish Sociological Association, 1989.

Konrad, G., and I. Szelenyi. *The Intellectuals on the Road to Class Power*. New York: Harcourt Brace Jovanovich, 1979.

The Koran. Penguin, 1977, trans., first published in 1956.

Kotarba, J., and A. Fontana, eds. *The Existential Self in Society*. Chicago: University of Chicago Press, 1984.

Krislow, S. "The Concept of Families of Law." In *Legal Systems and Social Systems*, edited by A. Podgorecki, C. Whelan, and D. Khosla. London: Croom Helm, 1985.

Kundera, M. *Immortality*. Translated by Peter Kuss. New York: Harper Perennial, 1992.

Laing, R. *The Divided Self*. Baltimore: Penguin Books, 1969.

Lanzmann, C. *Shoah*. New York: Pantheon Books, 1985, with introduction by S. de Beavoir.

Lemert, E. *Social Pathology*. New York: McGraw-Hill, 1951.

Levi, P. *Survival in Auschwitz*. London: Collier Books, 1961.

Lidz, V. "The Law as Index, Phenomenon, and Element—Conceptual Steps Toward a General Sociology of Law." *Sociological Inquiry* 49 (1): 5–25, 1979.

Łoś, M. *Communist Ideology, Law, and Crime*. London: Macmillan Press, 1988.

———. ed. *The Second Economy in Marxist States*. London: Macmillan Press, 1990.

Lukes, S. *Emile Durkheim*. Penguin, 1977.

Macaulay, Stuart. "Law and the Behavioral Sciences: Is There any There?" *Law & Policy* 6: April, 1984.

Machiavelli, N. *The Prince*. Cambridge: Cambridge University Press, 1988 (edited by Q. Skinner), originally: 1515–1516.

Marcuse, H. *One-Dimensional Man*. Boston: Beacon Press, 1964.

Marody, M. "Antinomies of Collective Subconsciousness." *Social Research 55* (1–2), 1988.

Marsella, A., G. De Vos, and F. Hsu, eds. *Culture and Self*. New York: Tavistock, 1985.

Mason, P., ed. *Totalitarianism*. Boston: D. C. Heath and Company, 1967.

Mead, G. *Mind, Self and Society*. Chicago: University of Chicago Press, 1934.

Merton, R. *Social Theory and Social Structure*. Glencoe, Ill.: Free Press, 1968.

Meyer, A. G. *Leninism*. Cambridge: Harvard University Press, 1957.

Milgram, S. *Obedience to Authority*. New York: Harper, 1974.

Miller, A. *The Obedience Experiments*. New York: Praeger, 1986.

Mlicki, M. "Towards Broadening the Concept of Social Traps." *The Polish Sociological Bulletin* 2 (94), 1991.

Morton, K. "Comments." *Newsweek*, Oct. 21, 1991.

Nakane, C. *Japanese Society*. Penguin, 1973.

Neumann, F. *The Rule of Law*. Leamington Spa, England: Berg, 1986.

———. *The Democratic and the Authoritarian State*. New York: The Free Press, 1957.

Neustadt, R., and E. May. *Thinking in Time*. New York: The Free Press, 1986.

New York Times. Interview with Mike Wallace. Nov. 25, 1969.

Nowak, S. "System Wartosci Spoleczenstwa Polskiego" (System of Values of Polish Society). *Studia Sociologiczne* 4 (75), 1979.

Nyiszli, M. *Auschwitz*. Frogmore, St. Albans: Mayflower, 1977.

Opatek, K., and J. Wróblewski. *Zagadnienia Teorii Prawa (Problems of Legal Theory)*. Warsaw: PWN, 1969.

Ossowska, M. *O Czlowieku, Moralnosci i Nauce - Miscellanea (About Human Beings, Morality and Science - Miscellanea)*. Warsaw: PWN, 1983.

Pareto, V. *The Mind and Society*. New York: Harcourt Brace Jovanovich, 1983.

Pawetczynska, A. *Values and Violence in Auschwitz*. Berkeley: University of California Press, 1979.

Peterson, C. "Totalitarian Law in Nationalist Spain." Paper presented during Sociological Conference in Madrid, July, 1990.

Petrażycki, L. *O Nauce, Prawie i Moralnosci (On Science, Law, and Morality)*. Edited by J. Licki and A. Kojder. Warsaw: PWN, 1985.

Piekarski, K. *Escaping Hell*. Toronto: Dundurn Press, 1989.

Podgórecki, A. *Zalozenia Polityki Prawa (The Assumptions for the Politics of Law)*. Warsaw: Wydawnictwo Prawnicze, 1957.

Podgórecki, A., and A. Kojder. "Ewolucja swiadomosci prawnej i postaw moralnych spoleczenstwa polskiego" (Evolution of the Awareness and Moral Attitudes of Polish Society). Warsaw, Polish Radio and Television Committee Poll, May, 1972.

Podgórecki, A. *Law and Society*. London: Routledge & Kegan Paul, 1974.

———. "Osobowosc Polaka" (The Personality of the Pole). Odra, No. 2, 1976.

———. "Calosciowa Analiza Spoleczenstwa Polskiego" (A Comprehensive Analysis of Polish Society). In Prace ISPIR, Warsaw, 1978.

———. "Intuitive Law Versus Folk Law." (Zeitschrift fur Rechts-Sociologie). Hefta, 1982.

———. *Program polityczny dla Polski (A Political Programme for Poland)*. Ottawa: 1982.

———. "The Three Levels of Operation of the Law." Ottawa, Carleton University, Department of Sociology and Anthropology Working Paper Series, 1983.

———. "Different Types of Legitimacy." Ottawa, Carleton University, Department of Sociology and Anthropology Working Paper Series, 1985.

———. *A Story of a Polish Thinker*. Cologne: Verlag fur Gesellschaftsarchitektur, 1986.

———. *Calosciowa analiza spoleczenstwa polskiego (A Holistic Analysis of Polish Society)*. In Materialy. Warsaw, 1987.

———. "Oppression from Within." Ottawa: Carleton University, Department of Sociology and Anthropology Working Paper Series, 1988.

———. *The Thoughts of Si-tien*. London: Poets and Painters Press, 1988.

———. "Sociotechnics: Basic Concepts and Issues." Ottawa: Carleton University, Department of Sociology and Anthropology Working Paper Series, 1989.

———. "Totalitarian and Post-Totalitarian Law." Ottawa: Carleton University, Department of Sociology and Anthropology Working Paper Series, 1990.

Podgórecki, A. *A Sociological Theory of Law*, Milano, Giuffre, 1991.

Podgórecki, A., and M. Łoś. *Multidimensional Sociology*. London: Routledge & Kegan Paul, 1979.

Podgórecki, A., C. Whelan, and D. Khosla, eds. *Legal Systems and Social Systems*. London: Croom Helm, 1985.

Podgórecki, A., Górecki, D., La Spina, A., Łoś, M., Olgiati, V. (co-editor), Peterson, C., Rolston, R., Sack, P., Schmidt, J., Shelley, L.; *Totalitarian Law*. Forthcoming.

Popper, K. R. *The Open Society and Its Enemies*. London: George Routledge & Sons, 1947.

Porozumienia Okraglego Stolu (Round Table's Agreements). Document by which the Polish Opposition and the Polish Government agreed in 1988 to abolish the Communist System.

Powers, C. *Vilfredo Pareto*. London: Sage, 1987.

Rapoport, D. *Assassination and Terrorism*. Toronto: Canadian Broadcasting Corporation, 1979.

Research Committee on Sociology of Law, 30 Years for the Sociology of Law. Onati, Spain: Onati Proceedings.

Riesman, D., with N. Glazer and R. Denney. *The Lonely Crowd*. New Haven: Yale University Press, 1961.

Ritzer, G. *Contemporary Sociological Theory*. New York: Alfred Knopf, 1988.

Romenesko, K., and E. Miller. "The Second Step in Double Jeopardy." *Crime and Delinquency* 35 (1): 1989.

Rose, Arnold M. was before and after World War II one of the leading figures in American sociology. He was, with Gunnar Myrdal and Richard Sterner, the co-author of *An American Dilemma*. New York: Harper and Row, 1944.

Sachs, A. *Protecting Human Rights in a New South Africa*. Cape Town: Oxford University Press, 1990.

Schmidt, J.K.H.W. "Roots of the Perversion of the Legal Order During the Third

Reich." (This paper was presented in Onati, Spain during the Sociological Conference on Totalitarian and Post-Totalitarian Law, June 21–23, 1992).

Shils, E. "The 'Authoritarian Personality' Expanded." In *The Authoritarian Personality*, edited by R. Christie and M. Jahoda. Glencoe, Ill.: Free Press, 1954.

Simmel, G. *The Sociology of George Simmel*. Glencoe, Ill.: Free Press, 1950.

Stanko, E. "Typical Violence, Normal Reaction: Men, Women and Interpersonal Violence in England, Wales, Scotland, and the USA." In *Women, Violence and Social Control*, edited by T. Hanmer and M. Maynard. London: Macmillan Press, 1987.

Steiner, J. *Treblinka*. London: Gorgi Books, 1969.

Steiner, K. "War Crimes and Command Responsibility: From the Bataan Death March to the MyLai Massacre." *Pacific Affairs* 58 (2), 1985.

Sykes, G. *The Society of Captives*. Princeton, N.J.: Princeton University Press, 1974.

Szczepański, J. J. *Malenka Encyklopedia Totalizmu (A Tiny Encyclopedia of Totalism)*. Krakow: Znak, 1990.

Taylor, T. *Nuremberg and Vietnam: An American Tragedy*. Chicago: Quadrangle Books, 1970.

Tejchma, J. *Kulisy Dymisji (The Inner History of Resignation)*. Kraków: Oficyna Cracovia, 1991.

Walker, N. *Sentencing in Rational Society*. London: Penguin, 1969.

Wedel, J. *The Private Poland*. New York: Facts on File Publications, 1986.

Wiesel, E. *One Generation After*. London: Weidenfeld & Nicholson, 1972.

Young, Iris M. *Justice and the Politics of Difference*. Princeton, N.J.: Princeton University Press, 1990.

York, G. *The Dispossessed*. London: Vintage, 1990.

Zawadzka, E. "Emigranci Nieustajacych Frustracjii" (Emigrants of Continuous Frustrations). Ph.D. diss. Polish University Abroad, London, 1991.

Znaniecki, F. *Ludzie Terazniejsi i Cywilizacja Przyszlosci (Contemporary Men and Future Civilization)*. Lwow, Poland: Ksiażnica-Atlas, 1934.

Index

About the Author

ADAM PODGÓRECKI is Professor of Sociology at Carleton University. He is the author of many articles and more than 20 books published in Poland, England, and the United States.